The Falklands
Crisis:
The Rights and the
Wrongs

Peter Calvert
Reader in Politics
University of Southampton

Frances Pinter (Publishers), London

First published in Great Britain in 1982 by
Frances Pinter (Publishers) Limited
5 Dryden Street, London WC2E 9NW

ISBN 0-86187-272-X

Typeset by Joshua Associates, Oxford
Printed by SRP, Exeter

'Take care, father,' said Bulloch gently, 'that what you call murder and robbery may not really be war and conquest, those sacred foundations of empires, those sources of all human virtues and all human greatness. Reflect, above all, that in blaming the big penguin you are attacking property in its origin and in its source. I shall have no trouble in showing you how. To till the land is one thing, to possess it another, and these two things must not be confused; as regards ownership the right of the first occupier is uncertain and badly founded. The right of conquest, on the other hand, rests on more solid foundations. It is the only right that receives respect, since it is the only one that makes itself respected. The sole and proud origin of property is force. It is born and preserved by force. In that it is august and yields only to a greater force. . . .'

Maël remained silent and motionless, with his eyes raised towards heaven; he felt a painful difficulty in judging the monk Bulloch's doctrine. It was, however, the doctrine destined to prevail in epochs of advanced civilization. Bulloch can be considered as the creator of civil law in Penguinia.

Anatole France, Penguin Island

Contents

Maps

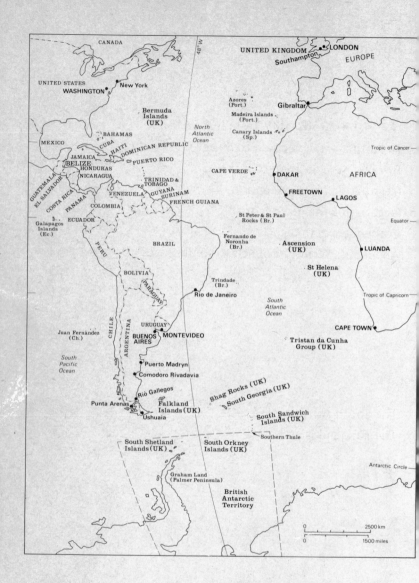

The South Atlantic Area

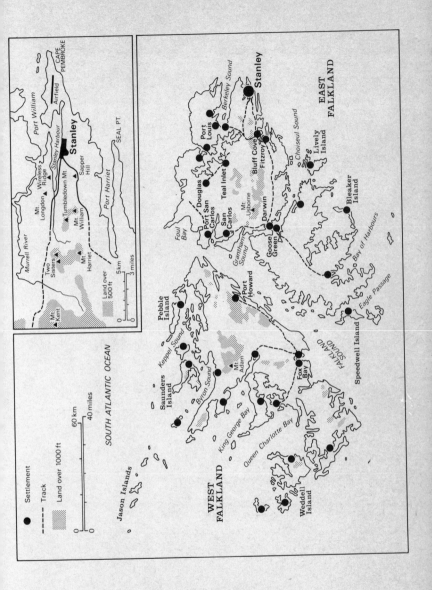

The Falkland Islands

1 'An island thrown aside from human use'

The Falklands crisis is first and foremost a dispute about sovereignty. Sovereignty is the fundamental concept on which the entire world order of the twentieth century is based. The crisis therefore has called into question the whole structure of that system, and it is not too much to say that the resolution of the crisis will affect the nature of the international world order until the end of the century and beyond.

But what is sovereignty? Sovereignty is a legal concept. It means that a government or person possessing it has sovereign, or supreme power: the right to do what it likes with the persons or things that it finds within the territorial limits it controls. It means ultimate power, not subject to any higher earthly authority. It comes to us today from an Old French word which came into existence in the Middle Ages.

In those days it was universally accepted that all earthly power came from God. Even then, however, there were various views as to how sovereignty was obtained. The idea lingered on that, on the model of the Roman Empire, there should be only one sovereign authority in the world, and that all other rulers should be subject to his authority. But this was successfully disputed by rulers such as Francis I of France and Henry VIII of England, and in any case it proved to be impracticable.

In the sixteenth century Charles V, who was both Holy Roman Emperor and also King of Spain and its overseas possessions in the Americas, was forced to divide his inheritance between two of his sons. At the same time the single spiritual authority of the Pope was also successfully disputed by Henry VIII. By 1648 Europe had become a set of separate states, each claiming sovereignty within its own territory, and the basis of the present world order had been established. But both before and since that time the development of that world order has been a continuous process, drawing from the past and contributing to the future in many ways, newer ideas and interpretations being added to the older ones without necessarily displacing them completely. So in the twentieth century former colonies have tried to achieve the same ideal of sovereignty held by the former colonial Powers, while people from all parts of the world have worked to try to bring peace to a warring world by creating new organisations for international cooperation, which by their very existence have changed and will continue to change the way in which 'independent' states behave.

The creation of a world of independent sovereign states was closely related to the expansion of Europe overseas and the creation of the great colonial empires. For in the absence of any supreme authority generally accepted as having the right to arbitrate between claims to territory the rush to acquire land and possessions brought about armed conflict on a global scale, though fortunately the capacity of the contesting parties to harm one another was then severely limited. The discovery of the New World was the most dramatic step in this direction. Its dangers were realised from the beginning by the rulers of Spain, and they took immediate steps to safeguard their claim to sovereignty over the new lands which Columbus had discovered and claimed on their behalf by the right of first discovery — then regarded as an obvious and clear claim to sovereignty.

At that time, in 1493, Portugal was the only other European power to have established overseas possessions on the coast of Africa and the route to India. To fix a line of demarcation between them and the new lands in the west, Spain appealed to the authority of the Pope, Alexander VI Borgia, himself a Spaniard, who established the line at a distance 100 leagues west of the Cape Verde Islands. In the following year, 1494, at the request of Portugal, the two countries signed the Treaty of Tordesillas, in which the line of demarcation was shifted 270 leagues further west to between 48° and 49° west of Greenwich (see Map 1), all newly discovered lands to the east to be Portuguese and to the west to be Spanish.[1] The consequence was that when, six years later, Cabral returned to Portugal and announced that he had discovered Brazil, it turned out to lie on the Portuguese side of the line. The conclusion is inescapable that the Portuguese already knew about the existence of Brazil when they signed the treaty, but very sensibly kept quiet about it.

Within fifty years the unity of Christendom had been broken and the universal authority of the Pope was no longer accepted. In any case the award was not accepted as universally binding, even by other Catholic monarchs. It was the devout Louis XIV who remarked that he had yet to be shown the clause in Adam's will that gave the King of Spain the right to rule half the world,[2] and by that time, the late seventeenth century, the British, French, Dutch and Swedes were establishing and expanding their own settlements in the Caribbean area and even on the mainland of South America, where at the same time Portuguese settlement had already overrun the line of demarcation of 1494. So keen was the competition for land that at the end of each in what seemed an endless series of wars, treaties were signed between the contending parties to try to regulate the position by mutual recognition. And time and again the next war brought a new reorganisation of territorial claims in line with the changing balance of world power.

When such treaties were drawn up there were already four grounds for claim of sovereignty competing for recognition. These were: the right of first discovery, annexation on either side of the line established by the Papal Award of 1494, occupation, or the actual effective possession and use of the territory in question (known to lawyers as *uti possidetis juris*), and cession by other Powers either formally by treaty or implicitly by failure to contest the claim. To these the French Revolution, with its mass mobilisation of peoples, was to add a fifth: the wishes of the inhabitants of the area under dispute, while in the course of time the difficulty of establishing the identity in any given case of a first discoverer has caused this principle to fall into disuse, in face of the rights conferred by the occupation or annexation of territory.

The wishes of the inhabitants are of course specifically

stated in Article 73 of the Charter of the United Nations to be 'paramount' in determining the right of any territory to 'self-government'.[3] Since 1945, with so many colonial territories striving for self-government, the majority of the world's independent states have consequently come to regard that principle as having more validity than the others. But this has in turn created new difficulties of interpretation. For there are two possible interpretations of Article 73. The strict interpretation holds that the colonial powers have a duty only to prepare colonies for 'self-government'. The loose interpretation, favoured by the members of the General Assembly, is that in this context 'self-government' means 'independence'.

To ensure that no claims by the inhabitants of any territory seeking independence should be overlooked, the United Nations established the Committee of 24 which we will come across again in this story. What it did not do was establish what should be done if the inhabitants of a territory, freely expressing their views, did not want independence. Nor did it establish that the older grounds for claiming territory had ceased to have effect. Hence the international law on the possession of territory, though well established on agreed principles and a large body of cases, is still subject to dispute and reinterpretation, and, since there is no overall authority to enforce it, it is still open for individual claimants to try to establish their claims by force and to seek to regularise them afterwards by international agreement.

With this in mind, we can now turn to the tangled history of the Falkland Islands.

The Falkland Islands consist of two large islands, East and West Falkland, and a number of smaller ones, with a total area of some 4,700 square miles (12,000 km²). They lie in the South Atlantic some 300 miles east of the island of Tierra del Fuego at the southern tip of the South American continent. Geologically their rock structure is unconnected with that of the mainland, and they appear to have moved into their present position relatively recently in geological time. Certainly, unlike Tierra del Fuego, they had no human inhabitants before the age of European exploration.

They were first sighted by sailors of the English ship *Desire* in 1592, and reported by her Captain, John Davis, as 'certaine isles never before discovered . . . lying 50 leagues or better from the ashore east and northerly from the Straits [of Magellan]'.[4] It was, however, nearly a century before the crew of another British ship, the *Welfare*, under Captain John Strong, made the first recorded landing on 27 January 1690, and named them after the then Treasurer of the Royal Navy, Viscount Falkland.

In the early eighteenth century the islands were visited more frequently, mostly by French sailors from the port of St Malo in Brittany, from which they came to be known in French as 'les Iles Malouines'. The so-called 'Spanish' name for the Falklands, Islas Malvinas, is in fact only an hispanised version of the French name, and a detached observer might well find it curious that a French name should be regarded throughout Latin America today as more Spanish than an English one. Indeed the absence of a Spanish name for the islands is the clearest possible proof that they were neither discovered nor settled in the first instance by Spain.

It was not until after the Seven Years War (1756–63), when Britain had made very substantial gains of territory at the expense of her opponent, France, and France's ally Spain, that the Admiralty dispatched Commodore John Byron (grandfather of the poet) to locate the islands and found a settlement and naval base. On 12 January 1765 the Commodore took formal possession of the islands in the name of King George III, and founded a settlement, Port Egmont, on Saunders Island off West Falkland. He had prudently sailed along the coast for over 400 miles and seen no trace of habitation, and with no communications it was a year later before the British settlers learnt that in 1764 Louis-Antoine de Bougainville, seeking new lands to compensate his country for the loss of Canada, had taken possession of and established a settlement on East Falkland in the name of King Louis XV of France.

Both acts were strongly resented by Spain. Although not known at that time, the islands clearly lay on the Spanish side of the line of demarcation of 1494. No doubt this claim did not weigh much with the French. But Louis XV was eager to please his royal cousin and ally. Accordingly in 1767

France relinquished its claim to Spain in return for an indemnity equivalent to £24,000, and the French settlement Port Louis, was renamed Puerto de la Soledad (Port Solitude).

It was now the turn of the British. On 4 June 1770 a Spanish frigate arrived at Port Egmont as advance guard for a fleet of five ships and 1,400 men and ordered the settlers to leave which, six days later, recognising the hopelessness of their position, they did. When news of the action reached Britain a strongly worded diplomatic protest to Spain threatened to bring the two countries to war. Ultimately, however, the Spanish Government at Madrid chose to disown the action, which had been ordered by the Governor of Buenos Aires, and to return Port Egmont to Britain, without prejudice, however, to the question of sovereignty.[5]

Only three years after the settlers returned to Port Egmont the settlement was closed down on the grounds of cost. It was the first time, but not the last, when the traditional tight-fistedness of the British Treasury was to contribute to diplomatic problems to come.[6] When the settlers departed they left behind them a flag and a plaque recording that the islands were the property of King George III. The Spanish presence on the islands lasted until the onset of the collapse of the Spanish Empire in South America, when Napoleon's capture of Spain itself forced the inhabitants of the colonies to make measures for their own safety and government. In 1811, a year after Buenos Aires had effectively become independent from Spain, the small Spanish garrison at Soledad was withdrawn and the islands left uninhabited once more, without, however, any indication of Spanish intent to reoccupy them.

Buenos Aires and the other provinces of the Rio de la Plata became fully independent in 1816, but it was another four years before the Government at Buenos Aires acted to establish a convict settlement on the islands. This act was disputed by Britain, whose command of the seas, ironically, was important in protecting the provinces from Spanish intention to reconquer them. It was a French merchant from Hamburg, Louis Vernet, who was chartered to establish a settlement and fisheries in 1826, and appointed Governor two years later, only to be recalled to Buenos Aires when he seized three United States ships in a dispute over fishing rights. In 1831 the Captain of the USS *Lexington* destroyed the settlement in reprisal, and deported the settlers, declaring the islands once again free of all government. A new attempt to found a convict settlement failed disastrously when the convicts mutinied and killed their Governor.[7]

At this point the British Government, increasingly conscious of the strategic importance of the islands to control of the route round Cape Horn, decided to exercise the rights of sovereignty which it had asserted throughout. The task was entrusted to Captain J. J. Onslow of the frigate HMS *Clio*. Arriving at Soledad in January 1833 he found fifty Argentinians under the command of Captain J. M. Pinedo of the Argentinian schooner *Sarandi*, and in a polite note acquainted them of his intentions and requested them to leave. At 9.00 a.m. the next day, 3 January, Onslow raised the Union flag on shore, and delivered that of his opponent to him politely wrapped up in a bundle. No force was used; the garrison yielded peacefully to the request to leave and did so two days later at the first favourable wind.[8]

From thenceforth until 1 April 1982 the islands were peacefully and continuously administered as a British colony, though the first agents of the colony, Mathew Brisbane and William Dickson, were murdered late in 1833 by some of the escaped convicts who were still at large. In 1834 the convicts were captured by a naval detachment, and the Royal Navy continued to run the islands until 1841 when a civil administration was established first under a Lieutenant Governor and later under a Governor. In 1845 the inhabitants gained partial self-government with the creation of both an Executive and a Legislative Council, in both of which, however, there was a majority of official, i.e. nominated, members. The colony, which after 1851 was developed economically by the Falkland Islands Company, received a grant in aid until 1880 and help with its mail service until 1886, but was thereafter self-financing. Full internal self-government was attained in 1951 after the achievement of full adult suffrage. New Constitutions were inaugurated in 1964 and 1977.[9]

Before leaving the early history of the islands, however,

it will be helpful to look at the various points which are relevant to the competing claims of Britain and Argentina, but it must be made clear that none of these events are in themselves an 'explanation' of the conflict of 1982. There are many other reasons for that, and it is these that this book sets out to explore. But precisely because the conflict involves the question of sovereignty, the historical grounds on which the claims to sovereignty rest have to be examined first.

As we have already seen, among the various grounds on which sovereignty may be claimed, actual effective occupation of territory with intent to act as sovereign is sufficient in itself. Britain has been in possession of the Falklands for much longer than most of today's independent states have been independent. It has established diplomatic relations with almost all the rest of the world's independent states, which in itself constitutes recognition of its right to rule the territories which it controls. Before 1 April 1982 only Argentina, of all these, had formally objected to its rule over the Falklands. But in the current state of international law, the question of recognition does not arise. As the Permanent Court of International Justice held in the *Eastern Greenland Case* only two elements are necessary to establish occupation: 'an intention or will to act as sovereign' and 'the adequate exercise or display of sovereignty'. There can be no doubt that Britain has fulfilled adequately both these requirements in the case alike of the Falkland Islands and the Dependencies, and on that ground alone that the Argentine claims would be held void, as were the French claims in the *Minquiers and Ecrehos Case* and the American claims in the *Island of Palmas Arbitration*.[10] It strengthens the British case before the United Nations and hence politically that Britain can demonstrate that at the last Legislative Council elections prior to the Argentine invasion, the islanders voted without exception for candidates who favoured the maintenance of British sovereignty.[11]

Argentine lawyers, on the other hand, base their claim almost wholly on events before 1833. They ignore the question of first discovery, since for them the Falklands, even if unknown, were already Spanish at the time: the assumption being that, under the Papal Award and line of demarcation of

1494, they were the sole and undisputed possession of that country from that time onwards. They next argue, as did the Government at Buenos Aires in 1820, that the rights of Spain passed to the United Provinces as successor state to the Spanish Empire, and further, to the Argentine Republic when it was constituted in 1853. Hence they regard what they persistently term the seizure of the islands by force in 1833 as an illegal act by Britain, contested at the time, which was belatedly rectified by the 'recapture' of the islands in April 1982.[12]

There are several weak points in this chain of argument, apart from the fact that it is asserted quite without regard for the grounds for the British claim. Spanish claims to the Falklands under the Award of 1494 were never accepted by other parties, and were specifically disputed by Britain. Unlike Spanish possession of Havana or British possession of Gibraltar, no formal treaty was concluded between the two parties resolving the question of sovereignty. In any case, any rights held by Spain, even if accepted, would not necessarily have devolved upon Argentina. A number of successor states took over the inheritance of Spain in the western hemisphere, and the question of which one obtained possession of any given piece of territory depended in the event on who was able to obtain and secure actual possession of it. A striking feature of Spanish colonial practice was that all its territories were regarded as coequal kingdoms owing allegiance to one monarch.[13] Hence when that monarchical link was removed, each was able to provide for its own safety according to the desires and actions of the local inhabitants. Even if the Falklands had formed an undisputed part of the former Spanish viceroyalty of Buenos Aires this would not necessarily mean that they should form part of Argentina today: if so Buenos Aires would equally be entitled to claim and to enforce its rule over Paraguay and Uruguay. Britain, having asserted a prior claim, is entitled to claim the rights of a successor state in the Falklands if it wishes to do so; indeed, if the Spanish claim has lapsed after the Spanish evacuation of the islands then the British claim must be admitted as having priority over any other.

Argentina's claim to be a successor state in the region is

partly based on the notion of 'geographical contiguity' — the notion that the islands, being off a mainland at present Argentine, should rightly be Argentine also. This principle has not been accepted in international law.[14] Historically, too, it is based on false assumptions. In 1833 there was as yet no Argentine control of Patagonia and Tierra del Fuego,[15] and it was to be some fifty years before that control was established by the Indian Wars of General Roca, and Patagonia partitioned between Argentina and Chile, which had previously claimed the whole of the region.

Lastly, Britain did not seize the islands by force, and under today's international law, the invasion of April 1982 could not be justified by any act or omission of 149 years earlier. Instead it constituted a deliberate and flagrant breach of the Charter of the United Nations, accepted by Argentina at its accession to that organisation in 1945.

The fact is that, although it is certainly true to say that Argentinian historians have long argued that the Falklands were properly Argentinian, the present dispute is relatively recent, and owes its origin to causes in both Argentina and Britain that have little to do with the Falklands as such. Since there is a considerable risk in discussing the complexities of the crisis that the Falklands and their inhabitants will be misunderstood or ignored, we will take a closer look at them before doing so.

The Falkland Islands themselves lie between latitudes 51° and 52° south and longitudes 61° and 57° west, and hence are as far south as southern Britain is north. Their mean annual temperature, however, at 5.6°C, is lower, owing to the strong westerly winds that blow throughout the year in those southern latitudes. Hence the climate, and the moorland scenery, resembles more that of Scotland and the Scottish islands, though the mean annual rainfall is comparatively low, only 635 mm (25 in) per year. Trees are scarce and the bare windswept grasslands have from the beginning of settlement been the main resource of the inhabitants, together with the abundant fish and other wild life of the deep and still relatively unexploited waters of the South Atlantic surrounding their broken and deeply indented shores.[16]

Early settlers from France in the eighteenth century introduced cattle which, when left to run wild, multiplied rapidly, and enabled the islanders to make a living from selling beef to passing ships. The British settlers, many of them Scots, began to introduce sheep, which they considered more suited to the countryside and climate, and in the last thirty years of the nineteenth century the wild cattle were systematically hunted down and the sheep population reached levels which have never since been exceeded.[17] Sheep cause serious erosion of grassland as they bite close to the ground level and their hooves break up the surface; the unique 'tussock grass' became virtually extinct and the best grasslands were damaged by overstocking. But the wool was of excellent quality, commanding a premium price on the world market, and the export of the wool clip has since that time remained the mainstay of the islands' economy. In 1971–2 it was estimated that there were over 634,000 sheep in the islands, and wool was exported in 1972 weighing just over 2 million kilos and worth £1,095,448. A further small quantity was earned by the export of hides and skins.[18]

But it is an old economic adage that 'sheep eat up men'. In the Falklands, as elsewhere where sheep have become the mainstay of the economy, the population has remained sparse and widely scattered, and other forms of agriculture have failed to develop. Apart from vegetables for their own use, the islanders, nicknamed 'kelpers' from the giant seaweed that grows round the shores, grow in the way of field crops only oats for the production of hay, and their main imports are of foodstuffs to give variety and interest to a diet that would otherwise be ample but monotonous. This is not because the growth of other crops would not be technically possible, and even profitable, but because of the dominance of sheep farming itself.

Like the Western Isles of Scotland, also, therefore, the islands have only a small population, and that has been tending to drop slightly since 1931. At 31 December 1972 the population numbered 1,957, almost all of British descent and 80 per cent of them born in the islands. Since then continuing political uncertainties and the shortage of educational facilities on the islands have led to a net outflow of population, and on the eve of the Argentine invasion of 1982 the residents, including people employed on short term contracts in the islands numbered 1,813.[19]

Of these only 500 were employed in sheep farming. The population, therefore, was heavily concentrated in the main settlement and since 1844 capital of the islands, Port Stanley on the east coast of East Falkland, with a population of about 1,000 (1,081 at the 1972 census). Of the remaining settlements, the largest, Goose Green on the narrow isthmus joining the two halves of East Falkland, had about 100 inhabitants. The rest were dispersed in a number of smaller settlements, outlying farms and islands; the countryside outside Stanley being collectively known to the islanders as Camp, and divided from the capital by thirty to forty miles of broken countryside, which made the easiest method of travel around the islands the light aircraft which could land freely on the many short grass airstrips. Unsurfaced tracks connected principal settlements.

The inhabitants of Stanley have traditionally been mainly employed in government services, shipping and trade, and the 1970s saw a considerable increase in the tourist trade both by air and from cruise ships doing a good trade in duty-free goods. There was no unemployment, and relations between the only trade union, and the employers, of which the largest was the Falkland Islands Company, were very good. Apart from the limited resources of entertainment, however, the principal factor driving Falklanders overseas was the limitations of the educational system, which was unable to extend to advanced secondary or further education. Free education up to the age of fifteen was provided in Stanley by government schools and outside by settlement primary schools, itinerant teachers, and a boarding and day school at Darwin on East Falkland, also catering for day pupils from Goose Green. In addition to this grants were made and annual scholarships offered to pupils attending boarding schools in the United Kingdom, Argentina or Uruguay. A postal lending library service operated in the outlying areas.[20]

Although the majority of children going overseas for education were naturally sent if possible to English-language schools in Argentina, the nearest place, the islands were not at that time strictly speaking dependent on Argentina for educational services, as will be seen. A similar position was also true with regard to medical services. The Government Medical Department provided a full range of medical services on the islands, including the maintenance of a thirty-two-bed general hospital in Stanley capable of dealing with all the main needs of its small community. For complex and difficult surgical procedures or medical conditions excellent medical care could be obtained in Argentina, if the patient was sufficiently strong to be moved, but again in normal circumstances the question of dependence hardly arose.

The islanders could keep in touch with one another and with the outside world by radio telephone, and receive news of themselves from Radio Falkland at Stanley and of the outside world by way of the South American service of the BBC. Although a number of them had relatives living in Argentina, and even forming part of the large permanent British community there, the islanders remained resolutely English speaking, clinging to the traditional way of life suited to their very different environment, though grumbling a certain amount at the scant attention that their remote possession received from the British Government they so loyally supported. It was only towards the end of the process of decolonisation of Britain's other territories, at a time when the question of Rhodesia was the principal post-colonial problem commanding attention in London, that the Government began to turn its attention to the Falklands, among its other few remaining territories.

It was for convenience pure and simple that in 1908 Britain placed under the jurisdiction of the Government of the Falkland Islands its other possessions in the South Atlantic and Antarctica, consisting at that time of South Georgia, the South Sandwich, South Orkney and South Shetland Islands, and the sector of the Antarctic continent lying between longitudes 20° and 80° west.[21] This apparently logical decision, too, was to have unforeseen consequences. For better or worse, the future of the Falkland Islands Dependencies, as they became known, was to be closely involved in the dispute between Britain and Argentina about the Falklands themselves.

It is doubtful whether 999 out of 1,000 of the inhabitants of the United Kingdom could have indicated South Georgia on a map of the world at any time before the beginning of April 1982. This sub-Antarctic island lies 800 miles (1,290 km) east-south-east of the Falklands. It consists of a massive ridge of volcanic rock, 100 miles (160 km) long and no more than 20 miles (32 km) wide, which rises steeply from the ocean bed into a series of mountain peaks from which great glaciers flow slowly into the sea. About half way along the northern coast, a deep inlet forms a fine natural sheltered harbour, Cumberland Bay, within which lies the capital of the island, the old whaling settlement of Grytviken, which latterly has been the headquarters of the British Antarctic Survey, which has a number of bases in the area, with a permanent civilian population of about twenty-five.

South Georgia was first discovered by a Spanish ship, the *Leon*, in 1756, but was formally annexed by Captain Cook on his second voyage (1772–5), in the course of which he was the first to cross the Antarctic Circle. Following his reports of enormous flocks of seals on the island, it became a staging post for sealers and whalers from both Britain and the United States, its fine natural harbours offering welcome refuge for their ships from the westerly gales. A permanent base on the island was first established in 1909, and civilian administration later placed in the hands of the British Antarctic Survey. Reindeer introduced in 1909 have flourished.

Some 470 miles (760 km) south-east of South Georgia again, on the edge of the Antarctic Sea, lies the uninhabited volcanic island group of the South Sandwich Islands extending over some 150 miles (240 km), from north to south. They were also discovered and annexed by Captain Cook on his second voyage.

Argentina's claims to these territories are very recent. It first claimed South Georgia in 1927 and did not claim the South Sandwich Islands until 1948 — curiously enough a year after Britain had offered to submit the dispute over other Argentine claims in the Dependencies to the International Court of Justice at The Hague. The offer was rejected, and in 1955, when the British Government approached the Court, as it was entitled to do, unilaterally, the Argentine Government refused to accept its jurisdiction. That complaint arose from Argentina setting up bases in Graham Land on the mainland of Antarctica itself, which was (and is) also claimed by Chile. But in 1959 the thirteen nations with interests in Antarctica signed the Antarctic Treaty, 'freezing' (appropriately enough) all claims to territories south of latitude 60°, including the South Orkneys and South Shetlands as well as Graham Land itself, for a period of at least thirty years from 1961. British territories lying within this region were, therefore, constituted for administrative purposes on 3 March 1962 as a separate colony, the British Antarctic Territory.

Argentine claims to these various areas have been based at different times on the concept of 'geographical proximity' (as in the case of Graham Land) and on supposed inheritance from Spain, though none of them were in fact claimed by Spain. Given Spanish emphasis on the line of demarcation of 1494 in other cases it perhaps should be mentioned that in any case South Georgia and the South Sandwich Islands lie to the east, that is to say, the Portuguese side, of that line. As for the claim to 'geographical proximity', that has no meaning in international law, and fortunately so. It would be hard to think of a principle more likely to lead directly to a third world war.

For the greater part of the history of the dispute there has fortunately been little practical reason for Argentina to wish to occupy the Falklands themselves. The reasons for the British Government deciding to make its claim over them effective in 1833 stemmed in the first instance from their strategic value as a naval base close to Cape Horn, commanding the gateway to the Pacific. Throughout the nineteenth century they remained the first point where ships damaged by the rough passage round the Horn could hope to secure dockyard facilities and repairs. With the arrival on the scene of the steamship, the value of the islands as a coaling station became no less important. Early steam engines were weak and inefficient, and by modern standards they consumed very large quantities of fuel. A world-wide naval power such as Britain therefore needed chains of coaling stations along the principal shipping routes, and it was the known value of the Falklands in this respect that in December 1914, led the German Admiral von Spee, fresh from the defeat of Admiral Sir Christopher Cradock at the Battle of Coronel off the Chilean coast, to attack the colony, as he had already done the British cable station at Fanning Island in the Pacific. While he was doing so his squadron of five cruisers was surprised by a hastily gathered British squadron under the command of Vice Admiral Sir Doveton Sturdee, and in the action that followed (8 December) four of the five, the *Scharnhorst, Gneisenau, Leipzig* and *Nürnberg* were sunk, with the loss of Admiral von Spee himself and 1,800 men.[22]

Argentina, with a southerly naval base at Ushuaia in Tierra del Fuego, did not need the Falkland Islands either to command the passage round Cape Horn or to gain access to the Antarctic, for which purpose, in the twentieth century, Britain came increasingly to rely upon South Georgia. Nor, indeed, were the islands' economic resources considered sufficiently impressive before the mid-1970s to warrant either Britain developing them or Argentina showing a keen interest in that aspect of something that had always been seen in Argentina as essentially a question of national honour and prestige. To understand the recent history of the dispute, and the onset of the crisis, however, it will next be necessary to have a closer look at the situation in Argentina itself.

2 Argentina—the decision to invade

Argentina is a country that has tragically so far failed to fulfil its promise. The reasons for this are not hard to understand, and it is one of the central ironies of this story that they are closely bound up with the country's relationship with Great Britain.

The provinces of the Rio de la Plata, the last to be colonised by Spain, were the first to proclaim their independence and, if Paraguay be included, the first to achieve it. The spark that ignited the movement for independence was the rash action of a British sailor, Commodore Sir Home Popham, who was sent with a powerful fleet to annex Cape Colony from the Dutch for the second time during the long Napoleonic Wars. Having heard of the efforts of Francisco de Miranda to secure British support for the independence of Venezuela, Popham believed that the Spanish colonists generally were ripe for liberation, and, on his own initiative and having nothing else to do, he set sail from South Africa for the Rio de la Plata with his whole squadron, taking with him the 71st Highland Regiment of Foot (later renamed the Highland Light Infantry) under the command of Brigadier General William Carr Beresford. The Spanish authorities at Buenos Aires were taken by surprise. The Viceroy, the Marqués de Sobremonte, fled from the town, which was occupied by Beresford's men on 27 June 1806. But hardly had the news had time to reach London than the people of Buenos Aires, angry at the failure of their leaders to protect them, rose in revolt and, with the aid of a militia force from the Banda Oriental (modern Uruguay), defeated Beresford's forces and captured their regimental colours.[1]

This action, known in Argentina as *la Reconquista* (the reconquest), marks the true beginning of Argentine independence. For though in 1807 British reinforcements were able to take Montevideo in the Banda Oriental, this merely spurred the people to disown their Viceroy and appoint the Frenchman, Santiago de Liniers, who had commanded the militia. When more than 10,000 troops sent out from Britain under the command of Lt Gen John Whitelocke attempted to retake Buenos Aires by storm on 5 July 1807 they were met by the massed resistance of the citizens on the flat rooftops. In the rain of cannon shot, bullets and missiles of every description the British forces suffered huge casualties. Having lost over 400 dead, 650 wounded and nearly 2,000 taken prisoner, Whitelocke was forced to accept terms which required no less than the total evacuation of the Rio de la Plata, for which, on his return home, he was courtmartialled and cashiered.

This second action, known in Argentina as *la Defensa* (the defence) ended British hopes of a foothold on the mainland of southern South America, but together the two 'English invasions' (*los invasiones inglesas*) had destroyed for ever the old dependence upon Spain. Then came the news of the French invasion of Spain itself, and the destruction of traditional authority in the mother country. The position of the new Spanish Viceroy became untenable, and on 25 May 1810 the council of leading citizens (*cabildo abierto*) came under pressure from a huge crowd in the main square demanding self-government under their own ruling junta (executive committee). They deposed the viceroy and followed the crowd's wishes, thus establishing – as it turned out finally – Argentina's independent control of its own affairs. Today the 25 May (*Vienticinco de Mayo*) is a great patriotic festival, and the square is named the Plaza de Mayo. For within a year the junta had disowned the Spanish monarchy itself, and by 1813 forces under one of the members of the first junta, General Manuel Belgrano, had decisively defeated the royalists at Tucumán and Salta, paving the way for the formal declaration of the independence of the United Provinces of the Rio de la Plata in 1816.

The irony was that the United Provinces were anything but united. Buenos Aires had led the way to independence, but the inland provinces had no wish to exchange rule from

Spain for rule from Buenos Aires, and the *gauchos* were prepared to fight hard and long to resist it. Ultimately they
were to find a leader of their own kind in Juan Manuel de
Rosas (1793–1877) who, having become Governor of Buenos
Aires with dictatorial powers in 1835, in the name of federal-
ism dragooned the inland provinces into unity by systematic
terror organised through his personal bodyguard and secret
police, the *Mazorca*. In addition he tried to recover Paraguay,
blockaded Montevideo for nine years, and incurred the
emnity of both the French and the British Governments.
But ironically, when he was overthrown in 1852 it was on a
British warship that he sought refuge, and he spent the years
of his exile in Southampton, first in the town and then farming a 300 acre farm in the Argentine manner at Swaythling,
about half a mile from the present site of the university.
It was at that farm that he died in 1877 and his remains still
rest in the Old Cemetery.[2]

When in 1853 the Argentine Republic was formally created,
it was Rosas who had created it in the name of opposing it,
though a civil war (1859) took place before Buenos Aires was
compelled to join it. In the latter part of the nineteenth
century, with the growth of the great meat packing industry
and its associated *estancias* (ranches), both Buenos Aires
and the inland provinces entered upon a period of remarkable
sustained economic growth. In this period, under the rule of
a powerful but constitutional oligarchy, the frontiers of
settlement were extended far to the south. Financed by
British investment a dense rail network was constructed
linking *estancias*, provincial centres and the capital. From
then up to the present immigrants have poured into the
country at a rate in any decade three times in proportion to
the population than that entering the United States, the
majority coming from Italy and Germany. Strongly influenced
by the anarchism of southern Europe, workers' organisations
grew up, and universal male suffrage, introduced in 1912,
brought the Radical Party to power. Despite strikes and
social unrest Argentina seemed in the 1920s to have made
the transition successfully to a modern democratic state
capable of handling its many problems, and to many it
seemed even that it was on the point of fulfilling the hopes

of the makers of the Constitution of 1853 and the generations since that it was destined to become the United States of South America.

In 1930 the dream turned sour. Argentina's economic modernisation looked much more complete than it actually was. The prosperity of the 1920s had been superficial, being sustained only by the massive export of one commodity, beef. The onset of the Great Depression hit it very hard, and the autocratic, incompetent and corrupt civilian government was an easy target for military conservatives determined to re-establish Conservative rule. A military coup in 1930 put a military dictatorship in power. Government intervention in the economy was established, and urgent negotiations begun with Argentina's biggest trading partner, Great Britain, to save the country from the catastrophic consequences of Britain's adoption of Imperial Preference, i.e. a system of tariffs on goods other than those from British territories, at Ottawa in 1932.

The result was the so-called Roca–Runciman Treaty of 1933, negotiated between the Vice President of the Republic, Julio A. Roca, and Walter Runciman, President of the Board of Trade, for Great Britain. By it, Britain undertook neither to reduce further its imports of chilled Argentine beef nor to levy new duties on Argentine imports for a period of three years. Argentina undertook in return to reduce her tariffs on British goods to those prevailing in 1930, to use sterling earned by her exports to the United Kingdom in the main only for remittances to that country, and to accord favourable treatment to British enterprises in Argentina. Blocked sterling balances were converted into a loan.[3]

To Britain the Treaty, renewed for a further three years in 1936, was a fair and reasonable attempt to help Argentina in its difficulties, in a way that protected the interests of the British investors and ranchers who had done so much to build up their country, and at the same time guaranteed the Empire's food supply.

In Argentina, outside Government circles, the treaty was almost universally disliked. The Radicals and those on the left strongly objected to giving favours to the British capitalists who, they said, were exploiting the Argentine people by high prices and bad service. To them the treaty was final proof of their belief that Conservative government was but the thinly disguised rule of the Anglo-Argentine 'ascendancy', evidence of whose influence, in clubs, social manners, business enterprises and way of life they saw all about them. Argentina had to them become in effect an informal colony of the British Empire. Nationalists on the right, equally, denounced the Treaty as a national humiliation. They were strongly encouraged by the effect of Nazi propaganda and the spread of fascist ideas, particularly in the ranks of the army officer corps, for in those years Germany was still the leading country for the supply of military instructors.[4] Both left and right, moreover, reserved some of their blame for the humiliation for the United States, who banned the import of Argentine beef for sanitary reasons and had now added high tariffs on Argentine imports, thus forcing the country into greater rather than less dependence on Great Britain. In the excitement both sides overlooked the fact that the Treaty did secure Argentina's primary aim of underpinning an economic revival that lasted into the first years of the Second World War.

It was the Conservatives who proclaimed Argentine neutrality at the outbreak of war. They had no choice, for many of those who did not actively support the Axis Powers did not expect the Allies to win, and after the United States had entered the war they and their followers were not prepared to follow the United States' lead in preparing for the defence of the hemisphere. The increased dependence on goods from the United States was in fact deeply resented, especially since the dollars needed to pay for them could not be raised by the sale of beef to Britain. As the military situation worsened, behind the façade of unity provided by neutrality, the strains increased to breaking point. In June 1943 a coup mounted by a group of younger nationalistic officers deposed the Government and in the name of Argentina imposed what was to be a frankly pro-Axis regime. For its aim was to do for Argentina no less than it appeared to them that Hitler had done for Germany: to make it, by discipline and obedience, within a space of twenty years, the leading Power on its continent.[5]

As far as their own political success was concerned, most

of these officers fatally miscalculated the international situation. As the tide turned in favour of the Allies, Argentina was forced first to break off diplomatic relations with the Axis Powers (1944) and finally in March 1945, only weeks before the end of the war in Europe, to declare war on Germany — the indispensable precondition for membership of the new United Nations Organisation being set up by the Allied Powers. The military government was almost totally discredited. Only one man, Colonel Juan Domingo Perón, who had taken advantage of his position as Secretary of Labour to force an alliance with the workers' movements he was thus able to control, emerged from the situation with credit. His political rivals had him arrested, but so great were the demonstrations in his favour that they had to free him. It only remained for the United States Ambassador of the day to declare his Government's opposition to his candidature on account of his pro-Axis record to make Perón the over-whelming choice of nationalistically-inclined Argentines for the Presidency in 1945.[6]

It was Perón who established the new pattern of Argentine politics by creating a mass political movement based on the support of the urban working classes, the so-called 'shirtless ones' (descamisados). Already more than half the population of the country lived in the capital, Buenos Aires, and mass rallies and demonstrations, using the Fascist techniques of the 1930s, kept them in a high state of political agitation. In this task he was strongly helped by his third wife, Eva Duarte (Evita), Argentina's leading film star, whom he had married on his release from prison, and whose well-publicised charitable works aroused strong emotional echoes in Catholic Argentinians.[7] Together they were a formidable team. Perón was in his younger days not only handsome and a vigorous sportsman, but an intelligent man who had read widely and could draw on a broad range of imagery and example in mak-ing the powerful speeches in which he aroused his audiences to an intense fervour in the service of the fatherland and the goal of making it the greatest nation in South America and a power to be reckoned with in the world at large. To a nation smarting with humiliation, the message was a heady one, and the people drank it up, eagerly.

It was Perón, therefore, who embarked at home on a programme of economic nationalism, symbolised above all by
the expropriation (with full compensation) of the British-
owned railway network. Blocked sterling balances were
used to pay off Argentina's foreign debt. Foreign financial
interests were taken over by the nationalisation of the
Central Bank, and investment directed into industrialisation
and the development of Argentina's still very primitive
agriculture, whose economic success had hitherto resulted
more from low costs than from high profits. As long as high
post-war demand for primary products continued, investment was also channelled into the development of the
oil industry, through the state owned YPF (*Yacimientos
Petrolíferos Fiscales*), and other prestige enterprises of less
economic value, such as the state owned telephone service,
airline and merchant navy. In the end, after the death of
Evita, his political touch deserted him. He was unable to
control rising forces of opposition in the army and the
Church, and in 1955 he was deposed by a military coup. But
by then he had had plenty of time to pursue his policy of
seeking greatness abroad as well as at home.

So it was Perón who, sensing the rising tide of decolonisation in the post-war world, revived the Argentine claim
to the Falklands which had so long slumbered in the pages
of the history books. To it he added new claims, never before
advanced by Argentina, to the South Sandwich, South Orkney
and South Shetland Islands, and to the greater part of the
sector of Antarctica claimed by Britain since 1908. As we
have already seen, Britain's offer in 1947 to refer the question
of Antarctic claims to the International Court of Justice
was rejected by the Perón Administration. Instead, when it
was announced in January 1948 that Britain was making
what appeared to be a major reduction in its naval strength
by the scrapping of five battleships, Argentina gave a pointed
hint about its wishes in regard to the Falklands by carrying
out naval manoeuvres near them under the command of no
fewer than five admirals. The British Admiralty responded
by dispatching the cruiser HMS *Sheffield* to the area to 'show
the flag'. A few months later the 'Argentine Antarctic', the
Falkland Islands, South Georgia and the South Sandwich

Islands, were all placed by Buenos Aires under the responsibility of a special division of the Argentine Foreign Office, which had in the meantime negotiated an agreement with Chile jointly to defend their claims in the region against Britain.[8] Invoking the aid of the United States, the two countries took their claims to the United Nations and to the Inter-American Conference at Bogotá. But the United States held to its traditional policy of not recognising any claims in the Antarctic proper, and in 1949 an agreement was arrived at between the three countries, renewed annually by a declaration, to keep military and naval forces out of the area south of latitude 60°, an agreement that was to pave the way for the Antarctic Treaty ten years later.[9]

The controversy of 1948 had been accompanied by mutual protests between Britain and Argentina about the setting up of Argentine bases in the disputed area, on the South Sandwich Islands and Deception Island, and as the bases remained, the protests continued annually. As his power began to wane, in 1954, Perón sought to revive the issue and with it nationalist feeling, by announcing his intention of 'saturating' Graham Land with Argentine settlers. Women as well as men were encouraged to go to Antarctica, so that children could be born there of Argentine nationality. It was as a result of this series of moves that Britain took its claims unilaterally to the International Court of Justice in 1955, when Argentina refused to accept its jurisdiction.[10]

So great was support for Perón that a trial military coup in June 1955 failed to dislodge him, though it made him once again dependent upon military rather than civilian support. Hence within months he was forced into exile by a combination of military and civilian pressures.[11] *Peronismo* — support for Perón's ideas — remained. It was now to split permanently between those who favoured the policies but not the man, peronismo without Perón, and those who sought the return of Perón himself, peronismo with Perón. Disappointment with the actual achievements of the period only acted to accentuate the strain of xenophobic, and at times irrational, nationalism which he had so successfully planted.

The army were deeply divided, too. A military President, General Aramburu, made deliberate attempts to eradicate peronismo and introduce an alternative route to national development by encouraging, not discouraging, foreign investment. His successor, the Radical Arturo Frondizi, continued his policies with boldness and established new links for Argentina with the countries of the Third World. But he was turned out of office by the military when he went too far and allowed peronista candidates to run in the elections of 1962. Fresh elections gave the presidency to Arturo Illia, a quiet country doctor. A modest man, he was to vanish almost without notice in 1966 when reviving military confidence led the generals to emulate the Generals in neighbouring Brazil and embark on a programme of militarily enforced economic development.[12]

The Brazilian programme was dramatically successful from an economic point of view — for years the annual growth rate exceeded 10 per cent. The Argentine Generals were much less successful. This was partly because their first leader, General Onganía, was a narrow-minded conservative who sought, for example, to tackle the problem of rebellious youth by sending out squads of soldiers to catch young men with long hair and give them a forcible haircut. It was also partly because the combined influence of peronista discontent and the influence of the Cuban Revolution had by this time given them not just one, but two armed urban guerrilla movements to tackle, and partly because they lacked any experts in economics, and were unable to find a civilian to do the job for them. In 1973 the Generals were therefore forced to allow civilian political parties to reform and to contest elections, with unexpected results.

The victory went to a close disciple of Perón. No sooner was he elected than he announced his intention of transmitting the power he had just won to Perón, who received the summons he had awaited for seventeen years in exile in Spain. Popular acclamation both for the decision and for the old man on his return was so great that the military did not dare to prevent it. Perón was even able to insist on having his fourth wife, María Isabel Martínez de Perón, a thirty-eight-year-old former dancer whom he had met in Panama, nominated and elected as Vice President.[13] Thus when he died of old age a year later, it was she, known popularly as

Isabel, who became the world's first woman executive President.[14] There could hardly have been a greater irony than the fact that she was called upon to rule a country famous — or notorious — for its cult of *machismo* (aggressive masculinity). During the years of Evita's power, Perón had been criticised by his enemies for according her 'masculine privileges', and they had succeeded in blocking her nomination for Vice President in 1951.[15] But Evita was a person of out standing political ability. Isabel was not. She owed her nomination, and her power, to the fact that by 1973 the bitterly divided Peronista following could agree on no one else, and the old man wanted no one else in the job who could challenge him, as she could not. Once he was dead she was quite unable to control the warring factions, and in 1976, faced with a country once more on the edge of economic collapse and torn apart by urban terrorism, the army once more stepped in.[16]

The Government of General Jorge Videla, President from 1976 to 81, has been associated above all with the massive programme of repression — the so-called 'dirty war' — by which the armed forces attempted to stamp out every vestige of support for armed terrorism. As in Chile following the fall of Allende in 1973, and in Uruguay after the 'soft coup' of the same year, there followed a wholesale attempt to hunt down the enemies of the regime in which torture was once again employed to instil terror as much as to disclose information, which by the nature of its source was in any case bound to be valueless. A particularly sinister feature was the mounting number of people who simply 'disappeared'. Estimates of the numbers of those who 'disappeared', and who have not been seen again (*los desaparecidos*), range from 10,000 to 20,000 or even higher, and in 1980 the newly-established Inter-American Commission on Human Rights presented to the Organisation of American States a report which named Argentina as the foremost country in the Americas for repression.[17] So firm was the military control of press, media and public expression that the only sign of open protest available was the weekly silent vigil of relatives in the Plaza de Mayo — the 'Mothers of the Plaza de Mayo'. By the beginning of the 1980s the campaign had however

ucceeded in its main aim, that of reducing overt military
hallenge to the regime to vanishing point.

The methods used, however, had presented the military
orces with a difficult problem of their own making. Tradi-
ionally, as we have already seen, the military in Latin America
ave intervened for relatively brief periods, to correct what
hey regard as immediate threats to the country, political
rder or to their own dominance. To this pattern Argentina
ad been no exception. In 1938, 1945, 1958 and 1963 the
rmed forces had withdrawn from the formal positions of
ower in favour of acceptable civilians or of public elections.
fter 1976 they did not. There had spread to Argentina
rom other Latin American countries, Brazil and Peru in
articular, the philosophy of 'military developmentalism',
r what at other times and places has been termed 'Nasser-
m'. This is the idea that the armed forces are uniquely
uited to carry out and to direct a programme of economic
egeneration, and that they must remain in power for so long
s is necessary for them to succeed in this task.

Argentina had long since learnt to live with rates of infla-
ion that would have staggered Europeans or North Americans.
Unlike other Latin American countries, their huge surpluses
f meat and grain meant that poverty to starvation level was
are, and to the outside world the disproportionately swollen
apital, Buenos Aires, wore an air of European smartness
nd sophistication. Beneath it, however, lay a critical depen-
ence on foreign exports of meat and grain, failure to diversify
he economy, excessive imports of luxury and consumer
oods which had to be paid for, corruption in high places,
nd an economic infrastructure living on borrowed time as
he investment of past generations slowly wore out without
eing adequately replaced. The world inflation of the early
970s accelerated the process of internal disruption. A major
isaster was the European Community's decision in 1975 to
top all imports of Argentine beef indefinitely. Not being a
ormer colonial territory, there was no transitional arrange-
ent for Argentina to cushion the shock. Inflation climbed
o over 300 per cent per year — an incredible figure which,
n practical, everyday terms, meant that government salaries
ad to be raised twice a month in order to keep up, and

shoppers raced round the supermarkets with their trolley
first thing in the morning in a desperate bid to keep ahead o
the staff making the daily changes in the price tickets!

The military government's response to this was predic
able: a fiscally conservative, monetarist solution whic
brought about rapid deflation and for a time brought infl.
tion down into double figures. Given the security climat
it did not have to worry about public criticism, still le
opposition. All political parties were dissolved, as were trac
unions, so long the mainstay of the peronistas. Congre
was dissolved and elections put off indefinitely; in fact
distinctive feature of the regime was its willingness to decla
firmly that elections were not even being contemplated. In
stead a Military Legislative Council was established, an
through the medium of a military junta of the chiefs of th
three armed services formal consultations took place wit
the officers of each as a kind of substitute for civilian cor
sultation. Ironically, as often with such military regime
pledged to carry out economic reforms, one area of skille
competence eluded them. An admiral in the previous militar
government proved no more competent at running th
economy than his civilian predecessors, and General Videl
gave the job back to a civilian who it was hoped might b
able (under military instructions) to do better.

In 1980 inflation began to climb again into three figure
The anti-terrorist campaign had been successful, but at th
cost of leaving General Videla and the military rulers dar
gerously exposed.[18] Once the major objective was achieve
political dissension began to be felt in the ranks of th
services themselves. But this time the military forces cou
not simply hand power back to the civilians. When the
opened talks with the Radical and other political leader
they found what they had feared, that they could not rel
on them for protection against retribution. Even if thes
politicians had the will there was no assurance that the
would have the power.

Military demands began to centre on two proposition
First, they wanted a future civilian government to enact
Law of Amnesty (*Ley de Olvido*), exonerating militar
personnel for all 'excesses' committed by them in the cours

f the anti-terrorist campaign. This was essential to protect individual members of the services from being prosecuted y the relatives of the dead and the tortured victims, many of whom had never been charged, let alone convicted of any crime. Second, sensing that if the civilians found themselves back in power, they might either choose, or be forced, to go back on any promise of an amnesty, they wanted a specific constitutional right to maintain military supervision over the cts of a future civilian government.[19]

To non-Latin American readers, this last requirement may well seem quite extraordinary. Military intervention is not a constitutional process to Europeans or North Americans. t is the reverse. But there have been and are Constitutions in other Latin American countries which contain specific provisions guaranteeing the rights and privileges of the armed forces, and according recognition to them as having special responsibility for the protection of the interests of the fatherland (*patria*). And all Latin American officers know of cases in which regular armies have been physically defeated y civilian forces. For a generation of them, the fate of the Cuban officers who went before firing squads in 1959 has erved to harden their resolve that the same fate will not befall them. For the Argentine armed forces in 1979 that esson had only recently been underlined by the success of the revolution in Nicaragua, and it is for that reason that they ave been so keen to lend not merely moral, but physical, upport to its opponents. In the last analysis, therefore, what they feared was not the civilians as such, but weakness and division among themselves. A Constitutional guarantee would serve as a support for the fainthearted in the event of another armed intervention being 'necessary'. In the meanwhile it would at least enable them more openly and easily o keep an eye on what was going on.

However, in the event they did not trust the civilians enough. It has to be admitted that military governments seldom get a good impression of civilians from the calibre of those that choose to work for them. It was therefore decided as a compromise to adopt a semi-constitutional position, by transferring the presidency to a new officer enjoying general support among the armed services who

could negotiate further moves towards civilianisation. I
March 1981 General Roberto Viola, who had been chose
in this way, took office, but during the winter the economi
situation continued to deteriorate to the point at whic
serious alarm was being felt about the country's ability eve
to service, let alone repay, its mounting short-term deb
It was for this reason that, in a last bid to save the militar
position, General Leopoldo Fortunato Galtieri, Army Com
mander in Chief, displaced him later in the year and assume
power at the head of the traditional triumvirate of the head
of the three services, or Junta. It was a crisis response to
crisis situation, and it destroyed the air of legitimate authorit
that the military governments since 1976 had been at muc
pains to try to build up. Before returning to have a close
look at this Junta and its members, however, it will b
helpful to look first at Argentina's traditions of diplomac
and the way in which the Falklands problem had develope
in the meantime.

Argentine diplomacy and the Falklands

In Europe and North America, it is hardly surprising tha
Argentina is seen as a land of Generals. But it is equally
land of lawyers. Characteristically such lawyers have sough
not merely a national, but an international field in whic
to work, and in consequence Argentine jurists have mad
notable contributions to the development of internationa
law and diplomacy.

One of them, Carlos Calvo, is famous for a prophecy h
made in 1864, and which is still to be fulfilled. 'The Argentin
Republic', he wrote, 'is called upon to be, within a ha
century, if we have peace, as considerable a power in Sout
America as are the United States in the North, and then wi
be the moment to settle accounts with that colossus with fee
of paper, the Empire of Brazil.'[20] In that year Argentina wa
once again involved in war, though not, as in the days c
Rosas, through its own choice. Instead the strange and tragi
President of Paraguay, Francisco Solano López, declare
war simultaneously on Argentina, Uruguay and Brazil, i
the pursuit of grandiose Napoleonesque dreams which wer

to lead in 1870 to his death in battle, the reduction of the male population of his country by nine-tenths, and losses of territory to the victorious powers, Argentina included. Since then, however, the Argentine Republic has not been engaged in a foreign war in any real military sense. Its participation in the Second World War, as we have already noted, was purely nominal, while the Brazilians, on the other hand, took an active part in Europe and gained distinction in the Italian campaign. It did send, though, troops to UN forces in the Congo.

The fact was that, when Calvo wrote, Argentina, with memories of British intervention in 1806, 1807 and 1845, was as much concerned with attack from Europe as from Latin America. It was Calvo himself who proposed a simple but effective means of reducing the possibility. In those days a recognised reason for the European Powers to intervene in Latin America was a dispute involving claims by a European company doing business in Latin America that its rights had been infringed by governmental action. It then sought re-dress from its home government. That government sent a warship and the dispute was settled — in favour of the company. Calvo proposed simply that all Latin American countries giving contracts to European firms should insert a clause in them (the 'Calvo Clause') by which the company renounced the right to call on its home government for support and voided the contract if it did so. Though at first European Governments, including Britain, refused to accept the validity of such clauses, they have now become standard practice.[21]

It was another Argentine jurist, the Foreign Minister Luis M. Drago, who in 1895 and 1902 urged the general adoption of an agreement preventing military intervention for debt collection in Latin America — the so-called 'Drago Doctrine'.[22] These ideas were later to contribute to the Charter of the United Nations and to that of the Organization of American States established in 1947. Argentina's prickly nationalism, and increasingly its distrust of the rising power of the United States, acted on the other hand to reduce the diplomatic effectiveness it might otherwise have held. Having joined the League of Nations as a foundation member in

TABLE 1: Heads of Government in Britain and Argentina 1963–82

	Argentina	Britain
1963		
19 October	Dr Arturo Illía	Sir A. Douglas Home
1964		
16 October		Harold Wilson
1966		
29 June	Gen. Juan Carlos Onganía	
1970		
8 June	Adm. Pedro Gnavi	
14 June	Brig. Gen. R. M. Levingston	
19 June		Edward Heath
1971		
22 March	Junta	
24 March	Gen. Alejandro Lanusse	
1973		
25 May	Dr Héctor Cámpora	
13 July	Dr Raúl Lastiri	
23 September	Gen. Juan D. Perón	

1974		
4 March		Harold Wilson
1 July	Sra. Isabel Martínez de Perón	
1976		
24 March	Junta	
29 March	Gen. Jorge Videla	
5 April		James Callaghan
1979		
4 May		Margaret Thatcher
1981		
29 March	Gen. Roberto Viola	
21 November	Maj. Gen. Horacio Tomás Liendo	
11 December	Vice Adm. (retd) Carlos Alberto Lacoste	
22 December	Gen. Leopoldo Galtieri	
1982		
19 June	Gen. Alfredo Saint-Jean	
1 July	Gen. Reynaldo Bignone	

TABLE 2: The Argentine Junta, 1976-82

	President	Army	Navy	Air Force
1976				
24 March	Jorge Videla	Jorge Videla	Emilio Massera	Ramón Agostí
29 March				
1978				
31 July		Roberto Viola	Armando Lambruschini	
1979				
25 July				Omar Rubens Graffigna
1980				
1 January		Leopoldo Galtieri		
1981				
29 March	Roberto Viola			
11 September			Jorge Isaac Anaya	
21 November	Horacio Liendo			
11 December	Carlos Lacoste			
17 December	Leopoldo Galtieri			
22 December				Basilio Lami Dozo
1982				
18 June		Cristino Nicolaides		
19 June	Alfredo Saint-Jean			
1 July	Reynaldo Bignone			

1920 Argentina withdrew from it in the following year when a resolution she proposed was not accepted. It was only after the outbreak of the Chaco War (1932–37) between her two neighbours Paraguay and Bolivia, that her Government decided to re-enter the League, rightly believing that to make use of that forum for diplomatic action would give her a degree of independence in negotiating a settlement favourable to her interests.

In that conflict, the only major war between Latin American countries to have taken place so far this century, Argentina backed Paraguay's claim to the disputed territory of the Chaco against Bolivia, which was supported by Chile. The Paraguayans were branded as the aggressors by the League for having officially 'fired the first shot'. Nevertheless in three years of bitter fighting they drove the Bolivians back to the foothills of the Andes and by doubling the size of their national territory, restored it to roughly what it had been before 1864. And no Argentine Foreign Minister since that time can fail to be aware that it was his predecessor, the lawyer Carlos Saavedra Lamas, who helped to secure that settlement for Paraguay by diligent diplomacy and procrastination that prolonged the war for two whole years. Nor that for doing so, he was awarded the Nobel Prize for Peace.[23]

By that time the Argentines' belief in their national desire for peace had already been well established. Its greatest and most famous symbol was the giant statue of Christ which was erected on the Andean frontier pass between Argentina and Chile following the peaceful settlement of their dispute over Patagonia in 1902.[24] At that time it was agreed that in future all other disputes between the two countries would be settled by arbitration, and the arbitrator was to be the British Sovereign for the time being.

So it was that when a dispute arose between the two countries over the desolate and uninhabited islets of Picton, Lennox and Nueva, in the entrance to the Beagle Channel on the southern shore of Tierra del Fuego the treaty of 1902 was invoked, though because of the Falkland question the Argentine Government agreed to accept instead the decision of the International Court. At the beginning of 1977 the

Court presented its award to the representatives of the two countries. It awarded possession of the islets to the holder, Chile. Immediately the Chilean Government announced its acceptance of the award. An ominous silence came from Buenos Aires. Almost a year later, the Foreign Minister, just as the deadline for reply was on the point of expiring, put on his Admiral's uniform and appeared on nationwide television to announce that Argentina was rejecting the award. On both sides warlike preparations took place. Troops were moved to Patagonia, reservists called up, and low-flying aircraft menaced one another's bases. War seemed imminent.[25]

At this point the Vatican offered its services as mediator between the two devoutly Catholic countries. On 23 December 1978 the offer was gratefully accepted. A year later the Pope's proposals were presented at a formal audience to the Foreign Ministers of the two countries. They proposed the creation of a 'demilitarised zone of peace' round the two islands, which, however, would remain Chilean.[26] The Chilean Government speedily accepted the proposals. The Argentine Government, regretfully, did not. To date, no proposals have been arrived at by the Vatican that are acceptable to both sides, though its efforts continue.

If Argentina has had little or no experience of modern warfare, therefore, the same cannot be said for diplomacy. Despite what many other countries regard as arrogance in its national pronouncements, its negotiators have shown considerable skill in the past, coupled with a strong determination to maintain established positions. All these characteristics reappear in the case of the Falkland dispute. But they appear to be magnified, as through the great distorting mirror of the national belief that the Falklands are rightfully theirs, and that the only problem is to get the world to recognise it as a fact.

As we have already seen, it was the charismatic Perón, in the days of his unquestioned power, who breathed new life into an old diplomatic grievance, and made the expansion of Argentina into the South Atlantic and the Antarctic regions a major part of his programme to get Argentina recognised as a Latin American and world power. Perón sought a 'Third Position', aligned neither with the United States nor with the Soviet Union, but heading a coalition of smaller 'uncommitted' states, and may in the future be seen as the first spokesman in the post-war period for what is now termed more tersely the 'Third World'.[27] It was he who sought to turn the issue of the Falklands into an anti-colonial crusade, though for the time being without success.

It was Perón's successor, General Aramburu, who found that however hard he tried to eradicate all other aspects of Perón's policies, the Falklands issue could not be avoided. It was, besides, a useful issue on which to rally national unity in the face of the enormous stresses generated by the internal conflict. It was he, therefore, who took the further step in a decree of 6 March 1957 of formally declaring part of the Territory of Tierra del Fuego not only the Falklands, but also South Georgia, the South Sandwich Islands, and the Antarctic territory previously claimed by Argentina.[28] By this decree the unfortunate inhabitants of the Falklands automatically became, in Argentinian eyes, Argentinian citizens: when they landed at Buenos Aires they were liable to income tax and military service. Not surprisingly, therefore, they were careful to keep away, with the result that direct communications with the islands by air soon had to be maintained over a distance of some 800 miles from Montevideo, the capital of Uruguay.

The next stage in the development of the issue came as the result of a private initiative. In September 1964 a nationalistic pilot flew his aircraft to Port Stanley, landed, and in a blaze of publicity proclaimed Argentine sovereignty over the islands.[29] The civilian government of Dr Illía, menaced from behind by the armed forces that had put it there, was in no position to resist the surge of nationalism thus generated. Later the same month the United Nations Committee of 24, where there was by this time a substantial majority of third world countries, took note of the incident, and recommended that the Argentine and British Governments negotiate about the claim.[30] The British Government demurred, but in December 1965 the General Assembly endorsed the Committee's decision in its Resolution 2065, which invited both governments 'to proceed without delay with the negotiations recommended.'[31] This was a substantial gain for Argentine diplomacy, for it supported Argentina's contention that there was indeed something to negotiate about, and so gave the formal recognition of the world forum to its interest in the islands.

In January 1966 the British Foreign Secretary, Michael Stewart, visited Buenos Aires, thus initiating the talks. In retrospect the decision to go to Argentina can be seen as a mistake on his part, since it placed the British Government at a disadvantage right from the beginning. And it was apparent that there was no meeting of minds. Mr Stewart explained that the British Government attached paramount importance (as stated in Article 73 of the Charter of the United Nations) to the wishes of the Falklanders themselves. He further pointed out that by its existing attitude the Argentine Government was making relations with the islanders more rather than less difficult. The Argentines, on the other hand, made it quite clear that they attached no importance at all to the wishes of the islanders. The islands were an integral part of Argentina and it was the wish of all Argentinians that they should remain so. They drew attention to the excellent conditions enjoyed by minority groups in Argentina, of which the substantial British community was one, and promised that the islanders had nothing to fear. Their interests would be fully respected by the Government of Argentina.[32] From the beginning, therefore, the Argentinians spoke of respecting the 'interests' of the islanders where the British spoke of respecting their 'wishes', and there is a world of difference between the two positions.

Since throughout the dispute the British community in Argentina has tended to take the Argentine rather than the British view of the Falklands, it should be noted here that the two communities differ in a considerable number of ways. Though the Falkland Islands have a *per capita* income about twice that of Argentina, the majority of the islanders are crofters and shepherds, living the normal sort of life of a remote British farming community. The 17,000 Anglo-Argentines form by contrast a wealthy – in many cases, very wealthy – sector of the upper class of their adopted country, their wealth in most cases deriving from the substantial ranching and meat-packing interests of the nineteenth century.

The former have chosen to remain British on British territory. The latter are expatriates in a foreign country, to whose culture their children and grandchildren have in many cases become almost wholly assimilated. For them the 'Malvinas question' poses a threat to their inherited advantages, and they are impatient that the obstinate islanders stand in the way of its settlement. The islanders regard the Anglo-Argentines, on the other hand, as tireless opponents of their right to determine their own future.

Before the talks could proceed further, two things made their progress very much more difficult. On 29 June 1966, the government of President Illía was impatiently thrust aside by the armed forces, led by General Onganía, a Conservative nationalist who was hardly likely to display much flexibility or imagination. Then in September an incident occurred which was to cause him the maximum possible embarrassment, and to precipitate the issue of the Falklands into the middle of the internal conflict that his Government was pledged to end. A group of twenty nationalistic students hijacked a DC4 airliner of the national airline Aerolineas Argentinas on a flight from Buenos Aires to Rio Gallegos with the new Governor of Tierra del Fuego, landed on the race track at Port Stanley, and proclaimed Argentine sovereignty over the islands. In those days air piracy was not yet commonplace in Latin America, as it was to become at the end of the decade, and Operation Condor, as the plot was known, created a sensation in Argentina, arousing massive demonstrations. Though the Argentine Government behaved very correctly, dissociating itself from the students, who were arrested, this was not until the British Government had dispatched HMS *Puma* from Capetown to show its determination to defend the islands.[33]

Since the talks were, as United Nations Resolution 2065 had required, between the two national governments, there was no provision for representation for the Falklanders themselves. Hence it was not long before the islanders began to develop a suspicion that the British Government might enter into some agreement with Argentina which they would have to accept as a *fait accompli*. Their chance came when Lord Chalfont said in the House of Lords that their wishes should be considered. To ensure that they were, in February 1968 the islanders sent an open letter to Parliament and the Press pointing out that they were not, at least not so far.[34] In response to this, the Foreign Secretary, Mr Stewart, stated publicly on 27 March that nothing would be done to change the status of the islands without the consent of the inhabitants,[35] a guarantee that was reiterated on 11 December following the visit of his special representative, Lord Chalfont, to both the Falkland Islands and to Argentina. At the same time, in separate communications, the two governments formally notified the United Nations that 'the area of divergence between the two governments had been narrowed'.[36]

Proof that this was indeed the case seemed to be provided by a major and significant shift in the Argentine position. This was the decision in 1969 to reverse the previous policy of making life difficult for the islanders, and instead to open up communications between the islands and Argentina.[37] This offered the British Government a series of possibilities for negotiated decisions which the Argentines hoped would lead to a diplomatic settlement of the major issue itself. Closer relations with Argentina, they believed, might in any case lead the Falklanders to accept the view of the British living in Argentina — that it was perfectly possible to live in Argentina and retain their British identity, as they wished to do.[38] This hope was shared by the Argentines themselves. They however had nothing to lose and much to gain by closer contact with the islands. For the time being it would show the people that their government was serious in pursuing its historic claims and prepared to do so in a friendly and just spirit. It would also enable valuable intelligence to be gathered which could be of value in the event of an eventual breakdown of talks.

During 1969, however, internal problems were to multiply in Argentina, as the effects of the Government's rigid austerity programme helped to consolidate opposition, both inside and outside the armed forces.[39] In July 1969 an unsuccessful coup in Córdoba showed that unrest had reached a dangerous pitch. It was followed by widespread strikes, which lasted into the early months of 1970.[40]

In face of these, General Alejandro Lanusse, who had

played a key role in engineering the coup of 1966, pressed for a return to civilian government, particularly after his friend, the strongly anti-peronist ex-President Aramburu, was kidnapped at the beginning of June. Onganía tried to dismiss him from his military post, but was himself deposed on 8 June.[41] General Aramburu's body was found on a ranch near Timbote, 240 miles from Buenos Aires, some six weeks later. His murder had put paid to widely expressed hopes that he might have served as a President of national reconciliation.[42]

With Onganía's fall power passed into the hands of a three man junta of the heads of the three services. Titular head was Admiral Pedro Gnavi, but the real power within the junta lay with General Lanusse and the army, and it was he who obtained the appointment as the new President (14 June) a political neutral. Brigadier General Roberto M. Levingston had served as an intelligence officer since 1947 and had risen to the command of the state intelligence service. At the age of fifty he was a rarity, a general who had commanded no active troops and had no political following.[43] Nevertheless, like many an Argentine military leader before and since, once in office he developed independent political ambitions, and when he tried to escape from the control of the junta, he was deposed (22 March 1971). Two days later Lanusse himself was appointed to the post, though on the understanding that he would share it on a rotating annual basis with his naval and air force colleagues.[44]

They were to be disappointed. Lanusse, a career cavalry officer, had been forced to take power himself as the result of rising terrorist violence on the left, involving the kidnapping of foreign businessmen and the assassination of a provincial military commander, among others. He remained convinced that a return to civilian government was the only solution and, after replacing Admiral Gnavi as a member of the junta in January 1972, he was able to remain in power to engineer the transition. His problem was to obtain a civilian leader without having Perón himself, who had been responsible for his imprisonment from 1951 to 1955. Candidates were therefore required to take up residence in Argentina well in advance of the proposed elections, and this Perón himself wisely refused to do.[45] The road therefore looked clear for a new candidate who would command the support of Perón without arousing the same inveterate hostility in both military and civilian circles.

Moves had already begun for the renewal of talks with Britain before the June 1970 coup. With three representatives of the islanders on the British Delegation, and a Conservative government returned to power in Britain, the talks began in July and resulted a month later in an Exchange of Notes concerning Communications and a Joint Statement. The agreement arrived at was explicitly made without prejudice to the question of sovereignty, and had seven main points. A joint consultative committee was to be established to discuss further questions arising between the two governments. Argentina would establish a special document, the so called 'white card', which would be the only document needed for islanders to travel through Argentina. They would be exempted from liability to taxes or military service in Argentina, both of which had previously been required of them. Britain was to arrange for a regular shipping service between the islands and the mainland. Argentina was similarly to provide for a weekly direct air service. Both governments were to cooperate in improving post and telephone services. Finally, the Argentine Government was to cooperate in matters relating to health, agriculture and education, including making available places for children from the islands in Argentine schools.[46]

In May and October 1972 the Lanusse Adminstration concluded two supplementary agreements, providing for them to establish a temporary aerodrome at Port Stanley and set up a regular air service, as envisaged in the earlier agreement. It came into operation in November the same year. At the same time the Government made it quite clear that they still wished to have talks on the issue of sovereignty itself. Talks were arranged in London in April 1973, again with representatives of the islanders taking part, but broke down when the British Government made it clear that they were not prepared to discuss the question of sovereignty.[47] But by that time President Lanusse's term was nearly at an end and in the next few months the political situation in

Argentina was to change with dramatic speed and unpredictability.

The elections in March were held in relative calm after a disturbed period inflamed by the brief return of Perón to Buenos Aires the previous November. The old man, regarded by observers as nearly senile, endorsed the candidature of his right hand man, Dr Héctor José Cámpora, and it was he who was elected and took office on 25 May, after Lanusse had retired from the service. Five died on inauguration day in clashes between demonstrators and police, in a wave of unrest that built up into the riots that attended the second and final return of Perón on 20 June, in which thirty-four were killed and 342 injured. Soon afterwards, under pressure from the trade unions and peronista elements in the armed forces, Dr Cámpora and his Vice President resigned together (13 July) to make way for their leader. It was the President of the Chamber of Deputies, Dr Raúl Lastiri, who as Provisional President, therefore, had the task of supervising the elections held on 23 September, which placed General Perón back in power with some 62 per cent of the votes cast. He and his Vice President, Isabel, were sworn in on 12 October.[48]

It was during this brief and very disturbed period that Dr Cámpora's Foreign Minister announced an important shift in Argentina's diplomatic position: adherence to the non-aligned movement.[49] As the case of Cuba has since shown, adherence to the non-aligned movement does not in any way act as a guarantee of non-alignment. But the declaration did in this case mean that the peronista governments that were to follow (1973–76) were to return to their leader's 'Third Force' position, and with it to his aspirations for leadership in South America. It also strengthened Argentina's position with regard to the majority in the United Nations Committee of 24, to which, by a letter to the Secretary General in August, the Argentine Government complained that it was Britain that was stalling on negotiations over the Falklands. The Committee, in Resolution 3160, declared that both parties should accelerate negotiations towards a solution of the sovereignty issue. But the debility of Perón meant that in practice little could be done. Meanwhile the internal

situation continued to deteriorate – in 1973 alone there wer
500 kidnappings, and violence spread, reaching further an
further down the scale of possible targets.[50]

When Perón died on 1 July 1974, of heart failure followin
a bout of influenza, machine gun emplacements were alread
established round the presidential palace. His widow, who a
forty-three became the world's first woman President an
the youngest head of state in Latin America, said that he
husband 'gave his life for national and continental unity' an
described him poetically as 'this great apostle of peace an
non-violence'. Her view may have been coloured less by th
events of his first term of office than by the fact that, follow
ing their first meeting, he had engaged her as a secretary t
type the book of his exile, *Force is the Right of Beasts.*[5]
Unfortunately her appeals for peace were not heeded. In th
next three months some ninety-three people were murdere
for political reasons. Stricter laws were announced i
September. In November a state of siege was proclaimed
and on 9 February 1975 the armed forces were called in b
the President to cope with the growing carnage.[52] By the
the Marxist Revolutionary Army of the People (*Ejercit*
Revolucionario del Pueblo – ERP) and the left-wing Peronist
Montoneros had already brought about the rise in oppositio
of the right-wing 'Triple A' (*Alianza Anticomunista Argentin*
– AAA), a militant right wing underground organisation tha
claimed in November 1974 to have killed more than thirt
left-wingers in the previous three months, and the countr
had moved in effect into a state of open civil war. In Decembe
newspapers urged an invasion of the Falklands by the wa
of diversion, and diplomatic relations were all but severed.

What saved the Government for the time being was th
residual effect of the name 'Perón' (her enemies tende
to refer to Isabel by her own surname, Martínez), and th
loyalty of the Army Commander in Chief, General Leandr
Enrique Anaya. Hostility was focused instead on Isabel'
closest confidant, Sr José López Rega, on whom she con
ferred extraordinary powers to coordinate governmen
departments. As inflation accelerated under the effect o
government attempts to buy support coupled with th
disintegration of central control, he was forced out of offic

11 July 1975) and had to flee the country. In the previous month alone the prices of all goods had doubled, and a few days before a furious Senator, who blamed him personally for the crisis, had challenged him to a duel. Prostrated with exhaustion, Isabel handed her powers over to the President of the Senate, and took a long rest in September and October.[53]

By the end of 1975 the Government had barely survived four days of military crisis when a group of air force officers rose in revolt and bombed the country's main air base at Morón.[54] In the end, as always, it was the Army that made the final decision, taking with it the previously loyal Commander in Chief of the Navy, Admiral Emilio Eduardo Massera. On 24 March 1976, in a bloodless coup, the President was deposed by the armed forces, who proclaimed their intention to carry out a 'national reorganization' and prosecute the war against the guerrillas.[55] The Junta of three, General Jorge Videla, Admiral Massera and Air Force Brigadier Orlando Ramón Agostí, appointed General Videla as President five days later, and soon afterwards formally constituted themselves as a permanent fixture in government by Law 25126, which provided that each member would hold office in the Junta for a term of three years.[56]

The disruption of government by the civil war and economic crisis of the previous two years had relegated the Falklands issue to a relatively low position in the scale of priorities. Despite Resolution 3160, formal talks were not resumed for the time being, though in September 1974 Mr James Callaghan, the new Labour Foreign Secretary, met the Argentine Foreign Minister in New York, and two further agreements were concluded, one to facilitate trade between the islands and Argentina, and the other to enable the Argentine national oil company Yacimientos Petrolíferos Fiscales — YPF, to market its products in the Falklands at Argentine prices.[57] Meanwhile persistent pressure from the islanders had persuaded the new government in Britain to send Lord Shackleton to the islands (January 1976) in order to prepare a report on the economic viability they might reasonably be expected to achieve. The consequences were comic, but they might have been tragic. The Argentinians strongly resented the visit, and a ship of their Navy, the destroyer *Almirante Storni* attacked the survey ship *Shackleton*, under the impression that its namesake was travelling on it.[58]

The Shackleton Report, published in July 1976, shortly after the Junta came to power, paid particular attention to the possibilities of offshore oil discoveries in the waters surrounding the Falklands.[59] Oil had been exploited in Southern Argentina and Tierra del Fuego for a long time. It seemed a natural deduction from the known facts to believe that there might be an eastern extension of the San Jorge and Magellan fields in the sedimentary basin, but in fact there had been no geological survey of the islands as a whole since 1924 and evidence from deep sea cores and seismic surveys in the region was by the mid 1970s still very limited. The first oil found off the Argentine coast had been located forty-five miles (70 km) from Comodoro Rivadavia in July 1970 by Compañía Agip Petrolera Argentina, a subsidiary of the Italian firm.[60] The report therefore had the effect of alerting the Argentine Government to these additional possibilities, and, while it would be a mistake to conclude as many British observers have tended to do, that in pursuing further the Falklands issue the Argentines were concerned with oil rather than with their 'rights' and their national honour, there can be no doubt that the thought that they might be being denied part of their national heritage was an important additional irritant.

The Shackleton Report also drew attention to the economic value to the islanders of having a permanent airstrip at Port Stanley long enough to take international flights from countries other than Argentina. The failure of the Communications Agreement to provide this was one of the deepest causes of suspicion among the islanders about British Government intentions. The Argentines had however done their share and provided the temporary airstrip and the air service. It was for the British Government to provide the permanent airfield, and it was at this unfortunate moment that the Treasury dug its heels in and refused to pay for an extension to full international length. Not surprisingly the Argentines also refused to pay. The British Government also failed to fulfil its undertaking to provide a regular sea service on the grounds that there was not enough demand. It was these physical constraints that drove the islanders most surely into a fatal dependence on Argentina that most of them profoundly distrusted, and which many British officials, drawing their impressions of life in Argentina from life among the diplomatic set and the Anglo-Argentine aristocracy, quite failed to understand. Treasury parsimony was to prove false economy indeed, for the airstrip remained too short to enable direct resupply of the islands from Montevideo or Ascension Island, and the costs saved were to be lost many times over in the campaign to repossess the islands.

For the time being, however, the Videla Adminstration was concerned first of all with national security at home, and secondly an economy running wildly out of control at an annual rate of inflation of over 300 per cent. Mention has already been made of the conservative economic strategy of Dr José Alfredo Martínez de Hoz, backed by the suspension of trade unions and the outlawing of strikes. Terrorism, too, was attacked on two levels. Some five to 6,000 suspects were rounded up and detained in punitive conditions, while special military courts were set up for terrorist crimes and subversion, and the death penalty reintroduced. At the same time undercover agents both inside and outside the regular armed forces meted out summary justice and assassination of real or imaginary enemies of the State.

It was therefore not until April 1977 that it was announced, following the visit of Mr Edward (Ted) Rowlands of the British Foreign Office both to the Falkland Islands and to Buenos Aires, that a new round of talks on the Falklands issue would shortly begin.[61] In the event much of the heat was taken out of these talks by the decision of the International Court of Justice, announced on 2 May, to award the disputed Beagle Channel Islands to Chile. This issue was to remain in the forefront of Argentine diplomatic concern throughout 1978, when the two countries appeared on the verge of war. What was not to emerge for over five years was that in March 1977 the British Government had been so urgently concerned about the possibility of an Argentine seizure of the Falklands that the Prime Minister, Mr Callaghan, had taken personal charge of the problem and dispatched a task force to the islands to make Britain's intention to defend them abundantly clear.[62] The Government also intervened to block a quite different threat: the possibility that by taking over the Falkland Islands Company Argentine businessmen might acquire control of the island's land and trade.[63]

The next round of talks between representatives of Britain and Argentina took place in Lima in February 1978, just after Argentina had rejected the Beagle Channel Islands award, and the prospect of conflict with Chile was pressing. In July President Videla retired and had to give up his membership of the Junta.[64] This enabled him as a civilian to remain as President for a term intended to be three years, but it was only one of a series of changes in cabinet and military posts which over the next two years were to mark the shifting balance of power within the military leaders, as they sought an enduring solution to the country's constitutional problems. The result was a 'political blueprint' under which General Roberto Viola succeeded General Videla as President at the expiry of his term, but remained fully restrained by the retention of the Junta. Another price for him, in turn, was to be succeeded on 1 January 1980 as Commander in Chief of the Army and a member of the Junta by General Leopoldo Fortunato Galtieri, who had risen to be Commander of the First Army Corps as recently as 29 January 1979.[65] General Galtieri thus became at the age of fifty-three the most powerful man in Argentina, and the power behind the Presidential Chair.

On 16 November 1979 Argentina and Britain decided to restore representation at Ambassadorial level in their talks, and a further round took place in New York from 28 to 30 April 1980 with a member of the Falkland Islands Legislative Council present for the first time.[66] The holding of these talks followed the return to power in Britain of the Conservatives under Mrs Margaret Thatcher in May 1979, and the appointment as Foreign Secretary of Lord Carrington, who had achieved world-wide recognition for his success in negotiating the transfer of power in Zimbabwe. But the talks did not, as the Argentines had hoped, give any hope of further movement on the issue of sovereignty. The new military generation of the 1980s were men who had spent their entire adult lives under the shadow of Perón. From youth they had been taught that the Malvinas were rightfully theirs. They did not intend their own civilians to have a free hand to make a mess of things again, and they certainly did not take a handful of Falklanders seriously. As the British representatives returned to the talks prepared to persuade the Falklanders that their future lay in closer relations with Argentina, the patience of the Argentines was beginning to run dangerously low.

The decision to invade

It seems natural to assume that a military government will want a military solution to a diplomatic problem. But the nature of the military role in government in Latin America is a complex one,[67] and the politics of the decision to intervene were correspondingly complex.

As we have already seen, military forces played a major role in the creation of modern Argentina over a period of at least seventy years. The armed forces therefore have ever since been identified, not just in their own minds, but in those of the public at large, with national freedom and national identity. Military leaders filled the vacuum left by the collapse of colonial authority. The armed forces therefore became the leading source of political leadership, and even civilian leaders necessarily drew on military support and military officers were always available to help in the subordinate tasks of government. In the twentieth century the professionalisation of military forces has merely acted to reinforce this dependence. Finally the introduction of universal military service has enabled the military forces to imprint successive generations of young men in their own image, reinforcing the almost unthinking acceptance of military participation in the political process.

Within the army — the dominant service — the key lies within the officer corps, forming about one-tenth of its 130,000 active strength. Its members, drawn in the main from the urban middle classes, enter it in their early teens on admission to military academy, and throughout these formative years their training is directed above all towards creating a strong sense of institutional loyalty. Since the military institution is the main thing, and possibly the only thing, that they have in common, it forms the principal bond between them, reinforced by personal loyalties to year-group and individual commanders, and strengthened by inter-marriage between army families, who in turn contribute an increasing number of cadets to strengthen the traditions of the service. A social institution of such strength that is not only armed but also, as a legitimate defender of national security, has the right to cloak all its operations in secrecy is in all normal circumstances more than a match for any other political organisation.

Such an army has, however, two weaknesses. These are inter-service rivalry and the internal divisions of politics.

First, inter-service rivalry, Argentina's naval forces also made a significant contribution to independence. Organised originally by an Irishman called William (Guillermo) Brown, they never lost their significance as defenders of the country against European incursions or menace from neighbouring Brazil and Chile, both states with substantial naval forces. At the beginning of 1982 the navy's strength exceeded that of the country's air force, an unusual position among the world's navies. Total strength including marines and naval air service was 36,000 men.[68] This gave it a relatively strong position in inter-service politics, reinforced since, lying as it does on the estuary of the River Plate, Buenos Aires would have good reason to fear the possible consequences of naval attack in a way that, for example, Brasília, capital of Brazil since 1960, need not.

But this strength was more important for internal than for external politics. Certainly in the particular case of the Falklands the 10,000 marines posed an obvious threat, since the Royal Marines were less numerous. But the Argentine ships were much less impressive,[69] the cruiser *General Belgrano*, having survived the Japanese attack on Pearl Harbor in 1941. The flagship, the aircraft carrier, *Vienticinco de Mayo*, ex-HMS *Venerable*, built 1945, was not so old, but its US Skyhawk aircraft were already dated. Of the nine destroyers, only the two most modern, British-built Type 42s ordered in 1970 and similar to HMS *Sheffield* and HMS *Coventry*, were really effective, as were three modern French-built frigates and two of the four submarines, small efficient German-built craft with very silent engines. The fact was that the dominance of anti-terrorist requirements in the 1970s had led to the Navy being relatively neglected among the three services, and though in the early days of the Videla administration the Foreign Ministry had been entrusted to an Admiral, the declining position of the service was marked by the change to a civilian appointment under his successors.

The air force was in a different position again. Like all other Latin American air forces, its development had been restrained by the self-restraint of the United States in forbidding the supply of military jet aircraft to Latin American governments up to 1969. Then the enterprising Swedes had succeeded in breaking the embargo, and the result was an arms race in which Peru, Brazil, Argentina, Chile and Venezuela all rushed to equip themselves with squadrons of jets, usually Mirage interceptors from France, but in the Argentine case mainly Skyhawks. Of bombers the air force had only nine elderly British-built Canberras. But its other aircraft were equipped to fire missiles, and the newest available, the French Super-Etendard of the Naval air service had just been purchased to make use of the French Exocet air-to-surface sea skimming missile, the potential of which had yet to be demonstrated in actual warfare at sea, despite being available to Iraq in the Gulf War. A large number of miscellaneous aircraft made up the apparently very impressive total of 223. Of these the only ones worthy of note, though, were the Argentine-built, propeller-driven Pucaras, which had been specially developed to fly slow, close to the ground for use in counter-insurgency campaigns against forces on the ground.[70]

Politically the relative standing of the air force could be deduced from the fact that, despite a total strength of 19,500 men, its Commander in Chief held only the rank of a Brigadier General (RAF equivalent: Air Commodore), meaning that he was always outranked by his army and navy colleagues.

The Junta created in 1976 was in itself the traditional embodiment of the formal balance of the three services, which in practice the rivalry between them constantly threatened to disturb. Maintaining inter-service balance was a vital supplement to maintaining the unity of each of the three services, because in a situation in which military services are highly politicised, it is imperative, if they are to survive, that they maintain unity above all else, and that this unity is not disrupted by fighting between themselves. Given the tight network of institutional ties, family ties and bonds of friendship between the officers of each service, such fighting — particularly if it were to result in the deaths of one or more officers — might well set up such a chain of feud and counterfeud that the survival of the institution itself would be threatened.

It is from this background that the typical institution of the military coup has emerged.[71] The coup is formally a military action. Troops advance. Tanks rumble through the streets. The President is escorted to the military airfield. Shots, even, are fired. But they are not usually intentionally aimed at anyone, the purpose being to preserve the honour of all involved by ensuring that the President surrenders only to overwhelming force. It has indeed been known for the President of one Latin American country in recent years to ask for a coup to be postponed for a day or two so that he could hold his daughter's wedding reception in the presidential palace.[72]

The same understandings exist to a degree between the services, but they are weaker, and there is always the danger they will break down. The fall of Perón in 1955, for example, was precipitated by a revolt of members of the air force, who bombed and strafed the presidential palace, the Casa Rosada ('pink house').[73] That of Allende in Chile in 1973 was triggered by disaffection among the navy. And in Argentina the divisions created by Peronismo run right through each of the services, where from time to time provincial or station commanders may try to force the hands of their superiors by rising in revolt. And, as we have seen, such problems were particularly likely to arise at a time when traditional loyalties were being strained by the prospect of a return to civilian participation in government.

Yet it was just this that General Galtieri, on his appointment in 1980, was expected to work towards. The appointment of General Roberto Viola as the military choice of

President could not have happened without him, and it was both preceded and followed by significant moves towards democratisation. And General Viola, when he took office on 29 March 1981, was no political novice. At the age of fifty-five he was a leading moderate, who as Chief of Staff in 1976 had helped to engineer the fall of Isabel, and had served as Commander in Chief and as a member of the Junta from August 1978 until December 1979, when he resigned to take up his nomination to the presidency.[74] Unfortunately for him he was to take office at a most critical time for the Argentine economy and three days after his inauguration, the peso had to be devalued by a massive 23 per cent. It had been devalued by 10 per cent only six weeks previously by Dr Martínez de Hoz, in an action he had resisted throughout the whole five years of his office.

The worsening state of the economy cast into doubt the whole economic strategy of the Junta so far. Worse still, that policy, the future of which was now so suddenly uncertain, had been deeply suspect to conservative military minds. Under it Argentina had been the only major country to oppose and to break the western grain embargo on the Soviet Union after its invasion of Afghanistan, and had indeed entered into long term commitments to supply grain to that country. On 22 April 1981, only two days before the United States lifted its own embargo, Argentina agreed to sell the Soviet Union between 60,000 and 100,000 tonnes of beef a year for a four-year period. Nationalist feelings were strong. Hostility towards the United States, always latent, was not assuaged by the decision of the Reagan administration to resume the sale of arms to Argentina which his predecessor had stopped. In fact the action probably emboldened the Junta on 25 March to reject the Pope's first proposals for the settlement of the Beagle Channel Islands question, which had been sent to both parties on 12 December 1980 and accepted by Chile on 8 January. By the end of April the arrest of two Argentine officers near Santiago on suspicion of spying had led the Argentine Government to close all border crossing posts and move troops up to Mendoza.[75]

The Argentine Government could not, however, escalate the conflict with Chile without breaking the solemn pledge not to do so that the Pope had wisely insisted on obtaining from both sides before starting the mediating procedure.[76] It could, and did, seek closer relations with Brazil. At the end of May President Viola and President Figueiredo of Brazil met on their frontier at Paso de los Libres, and issued a joint statement condemning all forms of 'interventionism' in Latin America — an obvious snub to the United States. But equally the two Presidents, as befitted their politically moderate position, also rejected two ideas dear to the ultra-conservatives in both armies: the creation of a 'Southern Cone' block (which would have included Chile, not welcome to Argentina) or South Atlantic Pact (which would have included South Africa, from which successive Brazilian governments, with their eye on Black African opinion, had been careful to distance themselves).[77]

President Viola, who had taken the politically hazardous decision to release former President Perón from the house arrest in which she had been kept since her fall, was also confronted by the consequences of democratisation, including, on 22 July, the first General Strike to take place since the military takeover. It was not a success, but, as it was illegal, the important thing was that it happened at all. Additional signs of change were the resumption in August of talks with the leaders of the long-banned political parties, and a series of changes in the Cabinet that testified to its internal division.[78]

In response there was a strengthening of hardline feeling within the armed forces. It was not long before this had its effects on the membership of the Junta, the crucial link between the government and the services. On 11 September, Vice Admiral Armando Lambruschini, a moderate, who had entered the Junta along with Viola in 1978, was succeeded by a 'hardline' nationalist and mystic, Admiral Jorge Isaac Anaya.[79] Then when, under the stress, the President suffered a mild heart attack and was taken on 9 November to the military hospital to recuperate, the Junta took control from behind the scenes.[80] To maintain the continuity of administration they had to choose a President *ad interim*, and the choice fell on another moderate the current Minister of the Interior, Major General Horacio Tomás Liendo.

Aligning himself tactically with the hardliners, who had been disappointed that one of themselves had not been chosen, Galtieri chose the moment to strike for power. Having taken soundings among the army, he met Viola on 11 December, and indicated that it was time to resign in his favour. Viola was in no position to refuse.[81]

Since Liendo declined in the circumstances to continue to serve as President, the job was again given to the Minister of the Interior, a post which had in the meanwhile gone in the inter-service bargaining to a representative of the navy, retired Vice Admiral Carlos Alberto Lacoste, who served until Galtieri himself could be sworn in formally on 22 December, with a full Cabinet already picked. But in the meanwhile Galtieri's position had been strengthened considerably by the appointment of the new Commander in Chief of the air force, Brigadier General Basilio Arturo Lami Dozo, to membership of the Junta, for with his support and that of Admiral Anaya Galtieri was able to become President without at the same time having to give up his own seat on that key body. For it was there and not in the largely civilian Cabinet that real power lay.[82]

There were points of interest, certainly, about that Cabinet. The most obvious was the appointment of Dr Roberto Alemann, a strong monetarist, to the revived post of Minister of Finance. Galtieri's succession thus represented a return to Videla policies, and was followed at once by the refloating of the peso and a cut across the board in public sector wages, including, significantly, those of the armed forces themselves.[83] This dangerous step was essential if a monetarist policy was to be effective, but it was one which was itself a measure of the anxiety with which the hardliners viewed the country's situation. At the same time the appointment to the Foreign Ministry of Dr Nicanor Costa Méndez represented acceptance of a policy he had been strongly advocating, close alignment with the hardline anti-Communist and monetarist policies of President Reagan in the United States, which Costa Méndez had visited twice in 1982.[84] Such a move was essential if the long-term position of the area were to be secured against the threat of conflict with Chile, and it seems clear that it was also intended as insurance,

to obtain American support for a militant policy with regard
to the Falklands also.

   For it was his Falkland policy that was the secret ingredien
in Galtieri's dangerous mix of policies. He had pledged him
self privately to take control of the islands by the 150th
anniversary of the British occupation, namely 3 January
1983. Classified official reports subsequently available
in Washington show that his Government began at once
well before the February talks, to prepare for 'the effective
occupation of the islands east of Cape Horn' and 'to define
by force the situation pending with Great Britain' as wel
as placing his country 'in a position of strength vis-à-vis
the pretensions of Chile to extend itself into the Atlantic
via the Beagle Channel'.[85]

   This was a policy from which no member of the Junta
can have dissented. Later, during the Haig mission, the three
men were described by one American observer (possibly Haig
himself) as 'a bunch of thugs with no one clearly in charge'.[86]
As regards the first charge, the three men were all career
officers in their early fifties: Galtieri fifty-four, Anaya
fifty-five, Lami Dozo fifty-three. Hence they had all served
through the unpleasant period of the anti-terrorist campaign
and had survived to reach high office. And no service was
immune from the effects of that campaign. Certainly many
army officers were tainted by association with the death
squads operating not only in the capital, but from a number
of provincial centres. But some of the worst reports of
systematic and prolonged torture of terrorist suspects –
many of them innocent of any charge – came from the Naval
Mechanical School in Buenos Aires which lies in the shadow
of the stadium where the World Cup Final was played out in
1978. The navy was, it seems, anxious to show that it could
be as efficient in anti-terrorism as the army, if not more so.
And as regards the second charge, service autonomy was a
protection against over-zealousness. Moreover the particular
advantage of the navy, and one that over the next six months
Admiral Anaya was to use to the full, was its ability to
operate away from home shores, where distance meant
independence of action.

   Belligerent statements regarding the Falklands in the

Argentine press had long been a feature of internal crisis. Hence the reports in *La Prensa* in February that the British were about to be presented with an ultimatum did not receive as much attention as they should have done. The latest in the long series of negotiating talks was due to be held in New York on 26 and 27 February 1982. The reports said that at these talks Argentina would demand the handing over of the islands. If this was not conceded, talks would be broken off and military action considered instead.[87]

In the event the talks held in the British and Argentine missions to the United Nations turned out to be peaceful. The British delegation, led by Mr Richard Luce, Minister of State at the Foreign Office on behalf of the British Government, included also Mr John Cheek and Mr Timothy Blake of the Falkland Islands Legislative Council. They reiterated their position that there could be no change without the wishes of the islanders, and it was clear that the islanders did not want change. The previous year the Argentine delegation made a strong attempt to persuade them. Speaking to them directly, they offered guarantees that the islanders could retain their traditions and local autonomy if they would accept Argentinian sovereignty. The Argentine Government would moreover, be prepared to put money into the development of the islands, and to give them a favoured status unequalled among its provinces.[88]

The Foreign Office, through a junior minister, Mr Nicholas Ridley, who had visited the islands in November 1980, had then already consulted the views of the islanders. He had made it clear to them that in the opinion of the Foreign Office the existing position was untenable. Argentina was becoming impatient, Britain was unable indefinitely to guarantee the defence of the islands, and no large-scale economic development of the islands was possible while the issue of sovereignty remained unresolved. The islanders had been invited to choose between four options. These were: a transfer of sovereignty to Argentina, a 'lease back' arrangement, by which sovereignty would be transferred but a lease retained by Britain on behalf of the islanders for perhaps ninety-nine years, a 'freeze' on the position for twenty-five years during which the Argentine links would be strengthened, or the ending of negotiations. They had chosen to ask for a twenty-five year 'freeze'.[89] It was this possibility that was now put again to the Argentine delegation. The idea of the 'lease-back' was not mentioned in the negotiations, though there is no reason to suppose that it would have been any more acceptable if it had.

The Argentine delegation, led by Dr Enrique Ros, Under Secretary for Foreign Affairs, and a career civilian diplomat, restated the Argentine claim to the islands, and spoke insistently of the need for quick results. The Argentines wanted a series of monthly ministerial meetings at which the question of sovereignty would be on the agenda. At the end of the two days, however, while the Argentine delegation referred regularly to Buenos Aires, a formula was arrived at for further talks with an open agenda, and the meeting broke up apparently in an atmosphere of general agreement.[90] In fact it has since become clear that the military hardliners in Buenos Aires had already discounted the talks as worthless. In their view Britain had for seventeen years been engaged in an endless process of procrastination and obstruction with the sole aim of denying Argentina her legitimate rights in her national territory. The British delegation's opposition to admitting the question of sovereignty as such was now confirmation to them that this view was right.

But what would be Britain's response to an invasion of the islands? Many military experts were inclined to believe that Britain simply did not have the capacity to resist. The British presence in the region consisted only of a small detachment of marines on the Falklands and an even smaller detachment on South Georgia, together with the symbolic presence of HMS *Endurance*. The announcement from London in July 1981 that as part of Britain's defence review, the *Endurance* was to be scrapped, seemed to indicate that the commitment to defend the Falklands was no longer taken seriously. The military, with their traditional notions of honour, considered that a decisive stroke would be regarded as a *fait accompli*, much as a military coup would be regarded by the losing party in their own country. Certainly in face of the Argentines' resolute intention to defend their own national territory, the islands, once lost by Britain, would not

be repossessed. The civilian Foreign Minister, Dr Nicanor
Costa Méndez, an ardent Anglophile, added the view that
Britain was 'too civilised' to use force in such an eventual-
ty.[91]

But Britain's intentions could be probed first. Three years
earlier an Argentine contractor, Constantino Davidoff, had
obtained a contract to dismantle the old whaling station at
Leith Harbour, north of Grytviken, on South Georgia, and
to employ Argentines on the job. On 19 March a naval
transport vessel, the *Bahía Buen Suceso*, delivered Davidoff
and his forty-one men to Leith, where they raised the Argentine flag. When the news was relayed to London by the
commander of the British Antarctic Survey in Grytviken the
following day, a diplomatic protest was made to the Argentine
Government that the landing, since it had occurred without
advance permission, was illegal. The following day the
majority of the men left. But a small group remained, while
British reactions were observed. Meanwhile the Argentine
patrol vessel *Bahía Paraíso* and two corvettes were dispatched
to give them 'protection', official confirmation of this
move being made over the weekend of 27–28 March.[92]
The rest of the Argentine fleet was due for joint fleet
manoeuvres with Brazil off Montevideo in Uruguay, and put
to sea on 29 March in full view of all. It required only an
order from Admiral Anaya to force the hands of his colleagues
by sending the Argentine fleet, already loaded with marines,
steaming for the Falklands. However there can be no doubt
that the Junta fully supported the action. Even as Dr Costa
Méndez was assuring the United Nations of his country's
peaceable intentions at 11.00 p.m. on Thursday 1 April,
Argentine forces were already coming ashore in the remoter
parts of the islands.[93] A Brazilian diplomat was afterwards
to express astonishment that the British Government had
ignored so many warnings of trouble to come. Never before,
he said, had the Argentine Government actually given notice
of its intention to resort to force. Three times in the previous
week the United States Ambassador to Buenos Aires had
visited the Foreign Ministry to urge the continuation of
negotiations.[94] He might have added, though he did not,
that the Brazilian naval command had been approached for

assurances of its support to its Argentine opposite numbers
in the event of an attack on the islands. Certainly right up to
the actual moment of the landings a clear sign from London
of the intention to deploy more than a token force on the
islands could have led to Operation Sovereignty being
aborted without loss of face. But as the days passed and that
order was not given, it ceased to be possible for such a force
however large, to arrive in time, and in any case to be on
the safe side, the South Georgia operation offered both
useful provocation and an effective diversion.

Once the landings had begun, of course, there was no
alternative but to carry them through. At 6.30 a.m. local
time on 2 April, troops landed at Port Stanley itself. They were
resisted by Royal Marines for some three hours, and suffered at
least fifteen fatal casualties in the battle. Ultimately, however
his forces heavily outnumbered, the Governor, Mr Rex Hunt
gave the order to cease fire in order to prevent further loss of
life. Refusing to shake hands with the Argentine commander
Admiral Busser (who was deeply offended), he was driven to
the airport in his official car, a maroon London taxi, and
deported to Uruguay.[95] Seven marines remained in hiding
until 5 April, when they were captured without injury, the
day before the official arrival of the new Argentine Governor
General Mario Benjamín Menéndez, to take up his official
duties. On the same day the twenty-two Royal Marines on
South Georgia were overwhelmed by a relatively enormous
force of Argentines, though not before they had killed three
of the invaders, destroyed a large assault helicopter, and
incredibly enough, inflicted serious damage on an Argentine
corvette with a Carl Gustav hand-held anti-tank missile
launcher.[96] On the same day, also, the first units of a British
task force sailed from Portsmouth for the South Atlantic. At
a moment of historic victory for the Argentine people, and
for their President General Galtieri, who took full credit for
it, there were few Argentines, if any, who took that news
seriously.

3 Britain—the decision to respond

Britain's foreign policy, Lord Salisbury is supposed to have said, is to float gently down river, putting out a hand from time to time to fend off from the bank.[1] In so far as foreign policy, unlike domestic policy, necessarily involves responding to actions over which one has no control, this description is accurate. In so far as it may suggest a relaxed and amateurish style of diplomacy, it is most misleading.

Britain in 1982 appeared in most respects to be the complete antithesis of Argentina. With twice the population (55 millions to 26 millions) crammed into one-tenth of the land area (93,000 to 1.08 million square miles) it was by world standards an advanced industrialised nation with a diversified modern economy. Uniquely among the world's advanced industrialised nations, it was self-sufficient in oil production and still retained in addition the huge part of the coal reserves on which its nineteenth-century prosperity had been based. On the other hand, it had for years been undergoing a prolonged and difficult adjustment to the post-industrial age, which had taken the unemployment level over the three million mark. The successive governments of the 1970s had in turn wrestled with the problem of inflation, which in each case their initial actions to please their followers had done so much to create, but at the beginning of 1982 the annual rate was again dropping steadily, if rather slowly, towards single figures. There were also economists to be found who suggested that Britain was leading the industrialised nations out of the recession of the previous years.

Britain had not been self-sufficient in foodstuffs since 1793, and so for nearly two centuries, despite the efficiency of her domestic agriculture, she had had to rely on vast imports from overseas, all of which had to be paid for by industrial output of manufactured goods. But since 1945 the rise of new industrial economies, such as those of Japan, Taiwan, Korea and Hong Kong, and the reorganisation of old ones, such as those of West Germany and France, had cut into her share of the world market. The need to export had thus been a main concern of all post-war governments, but in all fields from children's toys to advanced weapons systems the competition had grown fiercer and fiercer. Paradoxically the discovery and exploitation of North Sea oil, a stroke of good luck that had been vouchsafed to no other country in a similar position, had proved disappointing. Its revenues had been mortgaged before they had been received, its receipts fuelled inflation, and since its price was fixed in dollars rather than sterling the price of fuel remained remarkably high. Nevertheless the disparity between incomes was relatively modest by world standards, and Britain's people enjoyed a good standard of living and a degree of comfort never before available in the world's history to so many people at one time.

In foreign affairs, the dominant fact was that Britain, which in 1945 still ruled about one-fourth of the land surface of the world, had since then in a single generation granted independence to almost all of it. Most, if not quite all, of the countries that had gained independence during this period had done so peacefully, and Britain, which in the nineteenth century had fought more wars than any other country, had been at peace with the outside world since 1967. Since 1949 it had been a member of the North Atlantic Treaty Organisation, a permanent alliance of states to resist what was seen as the expansionism in Europe of the Soviet Union. The dominant partner in this alliance, the United States, had itself formerly been part of the British Empire, and shared a common language with Britain, kept continually up to date in British ears by the influence of first the cinema and latterly television. Though the 'special relationship' with the United States had had its ups and downs, it was generally accepted as inevitable. Since 1963, indeed, there were many who said that Britain's degree of dependence on the United States was such that it could no longer act independently in world affairs.

The first awakening to this possibility had come seven years earlier; in 1956, when Britain and France had supported Israel in a joint attack on Egypt designed to neutralise Colonel Nasser and his dangerous appeal to nationalism in North Africa. President Eisenhower's opposition to the action had been immediate, and faced with financial crisis the operation was abandoned.[2] In the following year, however, at Christmas Island in the Pacific, Britain, where the secret of 'splitting the atom' had first been discovered, became the world's third nuclear power. It was the dream that she could be something more, a major world power in her own right as in the days of the Empire, that was ended when the Macmillan Government in 1962 was offered and accepted Polaris, the strategic submarine-launched missile system, as its 'independent' nuclear deterrent.[3]

In the later 1960s things began to go very wrong indeed. The financial strain of maintaining the Empire had always been considerable, though it had always been British policy to make the colonies pay for their own defence wherever possible. But the costs of losing it had fallen fairly and squarely on the British taxpayer, and there was a general problem in addition of servicing an increasing debt for social and welfare expenditure on a declining industrial taxation base. It was the Wilson Government of 1964-70 that drew attention to the size of the debt in the course of its fight for office, and it paid the price of being unable to bring the situation under control by being 'blown off course' in its strategy for government-sponsored expansion of industry.[4]

The same government was also confronted with a decolonisation that had gone badly wrong. Since 1923 Rhodesia (now Zimbabwe) had been self-governing under a white minority government, which by 1965 was therefore in a position to resist any direct British pressure to concede majority rule, unless that pressure took the shape of a full-scale military invasion of the landlocked country. This seemed an impossibility. The Rhodesian Government thereupon proclaimed its unilateral independence, leaving the Wilson Government with the responsibility to do what it could to put the situation right. It chose to impose economic sanctions, backed by a mandatory resolution of the United

Nations, but the sanctions proved so difficult to apply that they took years to reduce the Rhodesian economy, even dependent as it was on exports of tobacco and other crops, to a sufficiently critical level to bring about political changes. Even then those changes only came about after a change of rule in the neighbouring states and a prolonged guerrilla campaign.[5]

Worst of all, in the heady year 1968, demand for 'civil rights' in other parts of the world reached Northern Ireland, and within a year part of the United Kingdom itself was shaken by the bomb explosions and sporadic assassinations of an active and vigorous terrorist campaign. The campaign and the measures needed to counter it went on relentlessly throughout the 1970s, resulting by the end of the decade in the deaths of more than 2,000 people. The images of these deaths and the destruction that accompanied them were flashed around the world, confirming the impression that Britain, like Argentina and so many other countries of that troubled decade, was in a state of near social dissolution.[6]

This was in fact not the case. But it was an irony that the most important post-war development, Britain's entry in 1971 into the European Community, was not recognised, save by a few very far-sighted observers, as the great political achievement that it was. There were many reasons for this. To begin with, Britain's entry was late. In 1956–57 the government had failed to recognise the significance of the events leading to the Treaty of Rome, and made no move to join. Instead it tried to organise a rival, less demanding economic association, saddled itself with obligations towards its new partners, and then announced in 1960 its intention to join the Community anyway. In the crucial year 1962 its application was not accepted, President de Gaulle of France giving as his reasons for opposing it the entirely accurate if uncomfortable observation that Britain did not really want to accept the Community's rules.[7] In 1964 the negotiations were resumed, but again failed, since Britain still saw the Community, and represented it to itself, as being about economic matters rather than about politics. By 1971 when entry was finally achieved, Britain was belatedly welcomed as a great political addition to a politically strong Europe.

But the great years of economic boom were then nearing an end, and after the oil crisis of 1973 had dealt a devastating blow to the British economy, it was very easy for those who had opposed Community membership all along to blame it instead. At the beginning of 1982 the Community was still widely unpopular in Britain, and the Labour opposition were pledged, if returned to power, to withdraw from it.[8]

This opposition to the Community had been greatly strengthened in 1979 by the return of a Conservative Government under Mrs Margaret Thatcher. The Thatcher Government, following the Heath Government before, drew its strength not from the traditional sources of British political leadership, but from the new rich, the self-made and the aspiring. Like their leader they demanded value for money, and they were determined to get it. Since 1964 the so-called Luxembourg Compromise, by which no decision touching the vital interest of a member state could be made without its agreement, had brought the political evolution of the Community to a standstill. Now by employing the same degree of complete intransigence that had previously been associated more with the French under General de Gaulle, the Thatcher Government set out to make such a nuisance of itself that the other members would be forced to concede what it wanted. The burden of its complaint was that Britain was being asked to pay too much for the privileges of Community membership, much of which was going to pay for the maintenance of the Common Agricultural Policy from which Britain benefited relatively little. In 1982, it was hoped, a permanent arrangement would be negotiated which would replace the temporary provisions which were the best that had been obtained so far.

Its risky policy towards the European Community, however, was but one aspect of the overriding aim of the Thatcher Government, to bring down the rate of inflation. The method of doing this had already been partially adopted by the Callaghan Government that had preceded it, namely to cut public expenditure by a policy of 'level funding' which necessarily involved a diminution of available services. It was inevitable that this policy — for long averted by the expedient of increasing public borrowing — would have to

take on board the crucial area of defence spending, though
this was both unpopular with traditional Conservative sup
porters in the House of Commons and contrary to Mr
Thatcher's election pledges, which had already resulted in a
3 per cent increase in planned defence expenditure. But at
the beginning of 1982 the Government had already incurred
enormous unpopularity by the severity, and often the ir
rational effects, of its cuts in other areas such as education
and social services, and its attempts to reduce the autonomy
of local authorities in order to control their expenditure
also. It was therefore inevitable that in his long-promised
Defence White Paper due in April, the Secretary of State for
Defence, Mr John Nott, would have to announce severe cuts
in defence provision.

The White Paper, however, was only part of a long-running
series of adjustments in the balance of defence needs and
defence expenditure. One of these, the announcement in
July 1981 that the ice-patrol vessel HMS *Endurance* was to
be withdrawn and not replaced, had drawn protests from
Falkland Islands representatives and the Foreign Office
that the action would be interpreted in Argentina as a signal
that Britain was no longer prepared to defend the Falklands.
Yet throughout the process of retrenchment the Government
had asserted continually its intention and ability to maintain
all its existing commitments, and in the White Paper itself
under the heading 'Beyond the NATO area', there was included
the significant paragraph:

In our statement on the Defence Estimates for 1980 to 1981, we discussed the need for the West to be aware of threats to its own and to
its friends' security in parts of the world outside the NATO area. We
also defined the three levels at which defence resources can be brought
to bear to protect our essential interests world-wide: assistance to
friendly states, preventative deployment to strategically important
areas and, in the last resort, intervention for deterrent or defensive
purposes. We confirmed in Cmnd. 8288 our intention to sustain and
where appropriate expand our activities on all three levels.[9]

As an official statement of Government policy the White
Paper had to receive the approval of the Cabinet. It was the
consensus of the political experts that since its inception in
May 1979 the Government had been dominated above all

by the personality of the Prime Minister. At the age of fifty-five, Mrs Margaret Thatcher, the first woman to become Prime Minister of a European country, had followed a conventional path of advancement. Born in Grantham, Lincolnshire, and educated there and at Somerville College, Oxford, she had entered politics from the presidency of the Oxford Union, had risen through the Conservative Party, and had served without particular distinction as Secretary of State for Education and Science (she was herself a research chemist by training) from 1970 to 1974. It was her courage in breaking with tradition at this point, and allowing herself to be put forward for nomination, that had enabled her to displace Mr Heath as Leader of the Opposition in February 1975. It was only a year since her predecessor had fatally misjudged the mood of the country and had called a general election, a year and a half early, in the middle of a miners' strike. But her choice expressed also both a belief among her supporters that previous Conservative governments had been insufficiently Conservative and a feeling that they had been weak in pursuing the objectives they set themselves.[10]

Mrs Thatcher's strong statements of opposition to the Soviet Union had earned her there the title of the 'Iron Lady', a title which, characteristically, she adopted as her own.[11] Once in power she did not go out of her way to meet the Soviet leaders, but neither did she go out of her way to challenge them. The successful conclusion of the negotiations that transformed rebellious Rhodesia into independent Zimbabwe were certainly aided by her standing among Conservative right-wingers, and the settlement, for which she gave generous credit to the Foreign Secretary, Lord Carrington, did nothing but good to Britain's standing among the non-aligned nations.[12] But the election of President Reagan in the United States found Mrs Thatcher ready to adopt the role of the staunchest and most loyal of the United States' allies, both inside and outside NATO, in a way that revived old suspicions of Britain within the countries of the European Community. Handling these and all other problems relating to overseas policy was the province of the Secretary of State for Foreign and Commonwealth Affairs and Minister for Overseas Development, Lord Carrington.

Peter, 6th Lord Carrington, holder of a Barony which had its origin in an Irish creation of 1796, looked to be and was in the classic mould of Conservative foreign secretaries.[13] An Etonian from an old landed family who had served with distinction in the Second World War, he owed his position, nevertheless, in the first instance to his own qualities, which had already led to his service in the Heath Government as Secretary of State for Defence. At the age of sixty-three, moreover, he was as he later said, doing the only job he had ever really wanted to do, and was respected as much abroad as at home for what Mrs Thatcher had termed 'the supreme negotiating skill' he had shown in the Zimbabwe imbroglio. Despite his deservedly high reputation, though, he posed no threat to Mrs Thatcher's leadership, since as a member of the House of Lords he was debarred from the office of Prime Minister by longstanding constitutional convention, and would in any case not have wanted to do so.

The combined Department of Foreign and Commonwealth Affairs had been formed as recently as 1968, when Britain's declining imperial commitments appeared no longer to warrant a separate department. The amalgamation was a measure of rationalisation which contained within it the basis for future problems. In the particular case of the Falkland Islands it meant that whereas previously the interests of the islanders were represented directly at Cabinet level by the Commonwealth Office, and those of good relations with Argentina separately by the Foreign Office, in the new Department, in which the Foreign Office tradition was dominant, policy with regard to the future of the islands would be decided internally. Within the Foreign Office, too, Latin America had traditionally had low priority as an area of concern.[14] British foreign policy was dominated by *Grosse Politik*, relations with and between the Great Powers, of which Britain, by her permanent membership of the United Nations' Security Council, was still at least an honorary one. The addition of Commonwealth responsibilities, with the accompanying very close and personal network of ties that it involved, had if anything reduced the amount of attention Latin America received.

Finally, by an irony, well into 1981 one issue in Latin

America had claimed urgent British attention. This was the Guatemalan claim to Belize, which had wished to become independent since 1969 and had been unable to do so because of the threat from its small but belligerent neighbour. But with the support of 139 votes to nil in the General Assembly of the United Nations, a majority which had taken the Foreign Office no little trouble to secure, even with the aid of the diplomatic efforts of the Commonwealth Caribbean countries, Belize had become independent in September without interference from Guatemala. And despite the presence there of several hundred British troops and a squadron of Harrier jump-jets, on a temporary basis, there was no long-term British commitment to its defence.[15]

Responsibility for the overall planning of Britain's defence, however, lay squarely with the Ministry of Defence. This had been created in 1964 by the amalgamation of the former War Office, Admiralty and Air Ministry, but until recently it had retained the tripartite structure corresponding to the three services it controlled, with a separate Minister of State for each service. When the Navy Minister, Mr Keith Speed, had been sacked for his protest at the proposals of Mr Nott's Defence Review, the Secretary of State and Mrs Thatcher had taken advantage of the occasion to restructure the second rank offices to eliminate service interests at the top level.[16] But the consequences of the review were much greater than that.

Mr John Nott himself was fifty in February 1982. He had served as an officer in a Gurkha regiment before reading law at Cambridge, where he had become President of the Union, and he was the senior of a group of younger Cambridge Conservatives who held positions in Mrs Thatcher's Government. He had served in the Heath Government, however, as Minister of State for the Treasury, and in Opposition as Opposition spokesman on Treasury and economic affairs. He was therefore very much identified as a supporter of Mrs Thatcher's economic strategy, and it was generally held that in sending him to Defence the Prime Minister had done so to ensure that the cuts in expenditure were sufficiently large.[17] Mr Francis Pym, who had been Mrs Thatcher's first appointee to the job, had not been so enthusiastic, and his talents were deployed instead into the formal office of Lord President of the Council and the real one of Leader of the House of Commons, the Cabinet post concerned with ensuring the safe and quiet passage of government legisation.

Mr Nott faced a daunting task. It was not to be expected that he would please everyone, but in fact he pleased practically nobody. His problem was that Britain's nuclear deterrent was obsolescent. In the twenty years since 1962 the American made submarine-launched Polaris system had been upgraded to make it more effective (Chevaline). But the British nuclear submarines that carried it could not take the latest system deployed by the United States, Poseidon, still less its planned successor, Trident, which had the capacity to outrun the latest anti-missile-missile systems deployed around Moscow by the Soviet Union. Trident was the best system available in the late 1980s, but it would be very expensive — US $7,500 millions at current prices — and it was really much more elaborate than Britain would need purely by way of a deterrent. As for other alternatives, Britain's airborne nuclear strike force, the V-bombers, were even older than Polaris, and there was no replacement in sight. Land based rocket systems, in as small a country as Britain, were also considered impractical. And the Cabinet members, being firm believers in the effectiveness of nuclear deterrence, were not prepared to heed the advice of their radical critics, abandon Britain's pretensions to be a nuclear power, and accept a second-rank role as a medium sized power with effective conventional defences only.

So it was decided to buy Trident. Unfortunately while still on the drawing board, the system had been further upgraded, increasing the cost to an alarming extent.[18] But in any case adoption of the system had crucial implications for all other forms of defence. It was therefore decided that Britain's role in the future would be purely as a member of NATO and confined to the immediate defence of the islands in the context of north-western Europe. There Britain was currently responsible for some two-thirds of NATO's naval defences in the region and the patrol of the air ways towards Norway, as well as the supply of a contingent to the British Army on the Rhine that had already repeatedly been reduced below levels that successive NATO commanders had considered barely adequate. Clearly something would have to go.

What emerged from the review was the idea of a newer, smaller, but – it was hoped – more powerful Royal Navy. Despite the example of the United States Navy, which had no fewer than thirteen giant ones, large aircraft carriers were to go; even the 19,500 ton HMS *Invincible* was to be sold to the Australians. Assault craft, too, such as the 12,000 ton HMS *Fearless*, would not be needed. On the surface, the new Royal Navy would consist of fewer small, light vessels, armed with the formidable Sea Dart and Sea Wolf missiles, such as the Type-42 destroyers and Type-22 frigates. Below it, it would depend on its nuclear-powered hunter-killer submarines, which could roam over vast areas at high speeds without ever needing to come to the surface and thus disclose their presence to the watching spy-in-the-sky satellites of the superpowers. It was the plans for this drastic pruning that had led to Mr Speed's protest, and as luck had it, the advance debate on the review was still arousing protests at the implications for shore establishments and the naval dockyards on the day, Tuesday 23 March, that Mr Luce was answering questions in Parliament on the landing of the Argentine 'scrap merchants' on South Georgia.[19] In fact, had the crisis erupted only a few months later, Britain's response would have had to be quite different, and the outcomes could have been quite different, too.

From negotiation to crisis

The British response to the South Georgia incident confirmed the Argentine Government in its belief that no serious resistance to a military coup would be made. It is necessary therefore to make two points clear at the outset. If the Argentines believed that, it was because that was what they wished to believe. If they interpreted British actions as confirming their view, this was because the British Government had been skilfully misled. The South Georgia incident was seen as it was meant to be seen, as an isolated provocative incident, not as the first move in a developing strategy.

Questioned on his statement in the House on 23 March,

Mr Luce was specifically asked by Mr Denis Healey, chief Opposition spokesman on Foreign and Commonwealth Affairs, if there was 'any evidence that this recent action by Argentine citizens took place with the support or knowledge of the Argentine Government'. He replied: 'The Argentine Government claimed that they did not know of the action which was taken by a commercial company. We have to note that the ship which transported the party there, though a cargo vessel, is a naval transport ship. That is something the House will need to note.' In response to a further question from Sir Bernard Braine (Conservative – South East Essex) Mr Luce restated the Government position on the Falklands as a whole to be unchanged. 'The Government,' he said, 'is committed to support and defend the islanders and their dependents to the best of their ability.'[20]

Pressed further, Mr Luce indicated that the forces available to take any 'firm action' that might be necessary consisted of 'a garrison of British marines on the Falkland Islands as well as HMS Endurance'. Though pressed to do so, however, he did not state that further forces would be sent, and in fact they were not.

What suggested that the incident was no more than a 'provocation', of course, was the fact that following, though not necessarily in response to, British protests, the Argentine ship and the bulk of the men it had landed had left South Georgia. It was not until 26 March that the Argentine Foreign Ministry revealed that the Bahía Paraíso had been sent to South Georgia to 'protect' the Argentines there, and not until two days after that that it was stated publicly in London that the Ministry of Defence was aware of the presence near the island of a patrol ship and two missile carrying corvettes the Granville and the Drummond.

At no stage was there a public statement in so many words by the Argentine Government of its intention to resort to force. Indeed subsequently the Foreign Minister, Dr Costa Méndez, was to be criticised by his own side for having neglected to take the elementary diplomatic step of formally breaking off the seventeen years of talks. It was only on Sunday 28 March that he officially refused to regularise the position of the South Georgia party, restating the Argentine claim to sovereignty, and told the British Ambassador at Buenos Aires that the diplomatic road was now closed. Consequently the realisation in Britain that an attack was imminent, and that it was aimed at the Falklands themselves, came very late and found HMS *Endurance* some 800 miles distant off South Georgia with a party of only twelve marines aboard to reinforce the garrison there. In this statement in the House of Lords on Tuesday 30 March, Lord Carrington informed the House that 'the Argentine Foreign Minister had said that the landing party in South Georgia . . . would be given the full protection of the Argentine Government', pointed out that the situation was 'potentially dangerous' and stated that it was his Government's aim to strive to work for a peaceful solution. It was made quite clear that the Government were prepared to defend the islands 'as effectively as possible'. But the statement appeared in the British Press the next day next to the report that Argentina's aircraft carrier, *Vienticinco de Mayo*, and its two Type-42 destroyers, the *Santissima Trinidad* and *Hercules*, had sailed from Puerto Belgrano, without any sign of it being realized that in the absence of immediate and positive evidence of effective military reinforcements being sent, the ability of Britain to defend the islands was negligible, and its willingness therefore might easily be disbelieved.

As Major Gareth Noot, commanding the marine garrison at Port Stanley, put it on 1 April, in face of an attack by the 140,000 strong Argentine army, the seventy-nine men of his command, even though they had been placed on alert, had only 'limited expectations' of success.[21] It was not until 4.30 p.m. that day that the Governor, Mr Hunt, called the heads of his Government departments together at 5 o'clock to inform them that the Argentine invasion force, headed by the *Vienticinco de Mayo*, was on its way to the islands, and that intelligence reports indicated the invasion could begin any time after 3.00 a.m. (local time) on Friday 2 April. And it was not until after the Governor had broadcast the warning of the invasion at 8.30 p.m. that Argentine radio stations started to announce that the force was on its way, that military leave had been cancelled, and that the islands would be in Argentine hands the next morning.[22]

Meanwhile Britain's Ambassador to the United Nations in New York, Sir Anthony Parsons, had requested the United Nations to intervene. The Security Council, on a resolution moved by the Chinese President, called upon both Argentina and Britain to refrain from the use or threat of force and urged both countries to seek a diplomatic solution to the dispute. Sir Anthony Parsons, on behalf of his Government, said that it would take heed of the appeal, but the Argentine representative refused to give any commitment, and by 12.30 a.m. on 2 April, Mr Hunt was able to tell the Falklanders that there was no indication of a change of course by the Argentine fleet.[23]

Argentines awoke the next morning to press and radio reports that the invasion was in full swing, as indeed it was. By 11.00 a.m. local time an official communiqué proclaimed that 'the Malvinas, Georgias and South Sandwich Islands' had been 'recovered', and called upon all Argentines to 'convert into reality the legitimate rights of a people which had been prudently and patiently postponed for almost 150 years'. 'It is not an invasion,' said Dr Costa Méndez, 'but the recovery of territory that is ours'.[24]

From these Argentine sources, reports of the invasion were already reaching London as the Cabinet met in emergency session. It was what was to follow in Parliament that strongly reinforced impressions that the Government had been taken entirely by surprise. First, at about 11.00 a.m. Mr Humphrey Atkins, senior Government spokesman on Foreign Affairs, said that 'appropriate military and diplomatic measures' were being taken in expectation of an attack. 'We shall sustain and defend the Falkland Islands to the best of our ability. As for the case of any invasion, I do not think it would be found to be easy,' he added.[25] In response to questioning from Mr John Silkin, the official Opposition spokesman on Foreign Affairs, who had pledged the Labour Party's support for resistance to any attack, he earlier answered a charge that in planning publicly to cut back the Fleet, the Government had brought the crisis upon itself — a charge that was only to be held in suspense following the further development of the situation into armed conflict.

'The right hon. Gentleman asked whether the Government

misjudged the situation,' he replied. 'The answer is "No". It has become increasingly evident over the past few days that the Argentine has assembled a fleet which was operating in the vicinity of the Falkland Islands. We have responded in the appropriate way, and I believe that taking the matter to the United Nations was the proper course.'[26]

Dr David Owen, a former Labour Foreign Secretary and spokesman of the fledgling Social Democratic Party expressed the hope that 'contingency measures' had been taken 'some weeks ago' to have naval forces in the area. Mr Atkins made no direct comment on this suggestion, but he did add a curious statement. 'The report on the tapes [that Argentine troops have landed] comes from an Argentine newspaper', he said. 'We were in touch with the governor half an hour ago, and he said that no landing had taken place at that time.'[27] The following day he was to correct this: the conversation took place at 8.30 a.m. and not at 10.30,[28] in other words, about an hour before the invasion troops actually started coming ashore at Port Stanley.

As ill luck would have it, public radio-telephone and telex links were inoperative during the crucial period owing to weather conditions in the South Atlantic, and in fact the first news that Argentine troops were actually ashore reached Britain through a radio amateur known as 'Bob'.[29] But this was not yet known when at 2.30 p.m., shortly before the House of Commons rose for the weekend, Mr Francis Pym, as Leader of the House, had to tell them that there had been 'no confirmation' of any change in the position announced by Mr Atkins. Mr Pym promised that if the reports were true, an emergency session of the House would be held the next morning, Saturday 3 April, and by then of course all the newspapers were full of it, though the situation was in some respects still very far from clear.

Outraged by a sense of national humiliation, and angered by reports of the military regulations that had already been imposed on the unfortunate islanders by the Argentine military commander, members displayed a rare degree of unity in the Commons' debate. Their unity, however, was for firm and resolute action rather than support for the Government, whose own supporters acknowledged that the debate was in most respects a 'disaster'. Yet it was this debate, and the need to present Parliament and public through it with a set of considered responses to the situation, which was to determine the entire future evolution of the crisis. Having failed to prevent the capture of the islands, the Government was now committed, in much less favourable circumstances, to free the islands from Argentine occupation at the earliest opportunity. Just how much more unfavourable was only to emerge later.

The Prime Minister, opening the debate, began with an account of the invasion drawn from a direct conversation with Mr Hunt after his arrival in Uruguay earlier that morning, and confirmed that there had been no civilian casualties.

The temperature rose sharply as she turned to the diplomatic history of the incident with the firm statement: 'I must tell the House that the Falkland Islands and their dependencies remain British territory. No aggression and no invasion can alter that simple fact. It is the Government's objective to see that the islands are freed from occupation and returned to British administration at the earliest possible moment.'[30]

She made it clear that bellicose comment in the Argentine press was not, in itself, a sufficient reason for sending reinforcements to the islands. Indeed, even after the South Georgia incident, on 19 March, the British Government had not wanted an 'apparently minor problem' to escalate, and had indicated its desire to achieve a peaceful solution, and the same low-key approach had been maintained, for fear of provoking the charge of war-mongering after the resupply of the Argentines on South Georgia on 25 March. On Monday 29 March, after the Foreign Secretary had offered to send a special emissary to Buenos Aires, intelligence had reported that the Argentine fleet was heading towards Port Stanley. At this point the Government had not only brought the matter to the attention of the Security Council, but through the Prime Minister herself had directly approached the President of the United States, President Reagan, to ask him to intervene directly with President Galtieri. 'We promised in the meantime', she said, amid uproar from all sides, 'to take no action to escalate the dispute for fear of precipitating the very events that our efforts were directed to avoid.'

Lastly, she indicated formally the means by which the Government proposed to make good its commitment to free the islands. 'The Government have now decided a large task force will sail as soon as all preparations are complete', she said. 'HMS Invincible will be in the lead and will leave port on Monday.'[31]

The Leader of the Opposition, Mr Michael Foot, said that 'so far' the islanders had been betrayed. 'They are faced', he had said, 'with an act of naked, unqualified aggression, carried out in the most shameful and disreputable circumstances. Any guarantee from this invading force is utterly worthless — as worthless as any of the guarantees that are given by this same Argentine junta to its own people.'[32] Yet a country which spent a greater proportion of its 'output' on defence than any other except the United States, to say nothing of its resources on diplomacy and intelligence, had been 'fooled', and the Government 'must answer for that.'

Debate centred on three points. Why had the government not had earlier intelligence of Argentine military moves? The point was made strongly by Mr Ted Rowlands, who as Minister of State at the Foreign Office in 1977 was in a position to state that the contents of Argentine telegrams lay open to the British Government. This question was not answered in the debate, though two days later sources in Buenos Aires were quoted as saying that the plans of the invasion had indeed been intercepted, and that they had been transmitted to London on or about Friday 26 March, that is before the Argentine force sailed from Puerto Belgrano for its 'exercises.'

Why had military counter-measures not been taken earlier, as a clear signal to Argentina of British determination to resist aggression? It fell to Mr Nott, the Secretary of State for Defence, to answer this one, and the way in which he did it led to calls for his resignation, along with that of the Foreign Secretary. He claimed, as was his right, that even if a 'large surface task force sufficient to deter or destroy the Argentine navy' had been dispatched immediately after the South Georgia incident, it could not have arrived in time to stop the invasion, though it 'might certainly have given pause to the Argentines'. He did not accept that it had necessarily been the Labour Government's decision to send frigates to the islands in 1977 that had stopped an invasion then. He went further, and at the end of his speech made an attack on Labour defence policy which threatened the structure of inter-party unity that had so surprisingly been manifest from the beginning of the debate on the central issue: the need to resist Argentine aggression. But even before that, his emphasis on the power of the task force to come had made it all the more paradoxical that he had not seen fit to deploy a much smaller proportion of it by way of precaution.

'It amounts to a formidable force which no other nation in the world possesses with the exception of the Soviet Union and the United States. If we were unprepared, how is it that from next Monday, at only a few days notice, the Royal Navy will put to sea in wartime order and with wartime stocks and weapons?', he declared. Later he added: 'I suggest that no other country in the world could react so fast and the preparations have been in progress for several weeks (sic). We were not unprepared.'[33]

If such preparations had in fact been going on for some time, it would seem only sensible to communicate some hint of them to the Argentine Government. In fact, as we have seen, actual military moves did take place during the crucial period, as the marine force was reinforced — an action hardly necessary if it were only to act as a tripwire, and likely to be misunderstood if, as was claimed at the time, it amounted only to the normal rotation of troops on station. Even after the Argentine fleet had sailed, it might have been intercepted by one of Britain's nuclear-powered hunter-killer submarines. The nature of submarine warfare, as was to be cruelly demonstrated later, makes a demonstration of its power very hard to use in a controlled manner. Yet a threat to torpedo ships actually engaged in landing operations might still have been made as a last attempt to avert the strategic disadvantages of local defeat.

The third area of contention, that the task force ought not to be sent, and that if sent it would be unable to repossess the islands in face of Argentine air attack, failed to develop in face of general desire for action of some kind and Mr Nott's confidence that the task force could do its job.

Doubts on this score were to surface afterwards, during the long period that the task force took to travel south to its station, and subsequently in each long interval in the military action. But at this early stage they were still swallowed up in a general feeling of surprise that Britain should have found itself in such a position at all.

There were many questions that naturally enough were not asked. Of all of them, however, the one that members might have found it most salutary to review was the question of why Mrs Thatcher had placed such confidence in the intervention of President Reagan. The President did, as he had promised, telephone President Galtieri directly, and talked to him for three-quarters of an hour, urging him, in vain, to avoid the use of force. He had hinted that Britain would be prepared to use force in return, and, according to Washington officials, made it clear that Mrs Thatcher was 'a determined person' who would not give in.[34] But given Argentine assumptions the use of President Reagan as an intermediary was more likely to be construed as evidence of British weakness than British strength. In any case, with the fleet on the high seas, its recall was not likely to be secured by anything less than notice of deployment of United States forces to resist further action — something which in the post-Vietnam era of the 'imperilled Presidency' was quite out of the question. Resort to Washington, therefore, was a fatal waste of time.

Resort to New York was another matter. Mr Foot made much in his speech, and was to make more subsequently, of the importance to Britain of involving the United Nations in the question as soon and as fully as possible. At the time his call, one bound to rally support from all sides of the bitterly divided Labour Party, seemed to some observers to have little other purpose to serve. Even in New York it did not look as though Britain, as an old colonial Power engaged in a struggle for a colonial possession, could get the nine votes in the Security Council for a condemnation of Argentina. Even if it did, the Argentines themselves believed that the Soviet Union, needing their grain supplies, would veto it.

Both beliefs turned out to be wrong. The vigorous diplomacy of Sir Anthony Parsons and the British team at the United Nations found an unexpectedly favourable response, helped by the strong statements against the Argentine aggression made by France and Ireland. The very fact that both these countries were ones with which Britain had long-running diplomatic disputes, the former over Britain's contributions to the Community and the latter over its policy in Northern Ireland, made their support doubly welcome. Reports circulating among delegates that Argentine troops might already have been on the Falklands when Dr Costa Méndez was affirming his country's desire for peace to the Security Council on the evening of 1 April raised serious doubts, in some delegations for the first time, about Argentine veracity. Then, in the event, Resolution 502, drafted by Sir Anthony, when put to the Council, was supported by ten members and received only one negative vote: that of Panama, which alone of the members of the Council had supported the Argentine position. The Soviet Union abstained.[35]

The resolution had three parts. It called for an immediate cessation of hostilities, for the immediate withdrawal of Argentine forces from the islands, and for Britain and Argentina to settle their disputes peacefully in accordance with the Charter of the United Nations. This last point of reference to Article 2(4) of the Charter prohibiting the use of force against the territorial integrity of any state, as well as to Article 2(3) requiring disputes between states to be settled by peaceful means.[36]

Britain gratefully accepted this resolution as a vindication of its position, and in the months to come it was used extensively as a justification for further British action, including military action. The dispatch of the task force had indeed already been justified by Mr Nott to the British House of Commons under Article 51 of the Charter, which guarantees to each and every nation the 'inherent right' of self-defence, which, being inherent, needs no formal resolution of the United Nations, provided that the use of force is maintained as proportionate to the force used by the attacker. But the British Government saw Argentine failure to comply with the provision of Resolution 502 calling for its withdrawal from the islands as additional support for its own use of force. It was, moreover, encouraged to do so by a very uncompromising statement from Buenos Aires just after midnight on Sunday 4 April, in which, only hours after the Security Council resolution, President Galtieri stated that Argentina's interest and honour were not negotiable and that his country would retain its freedom of action.[37]

Seen from the Argentine point of view, the islands were Argentine territory. They were not required to withdraw from them, but Britain, on the other hand, was enjoined not to use force. The Argentine Foreign Ministry, proclaiming that (the islands now having been taken) they were and had been all along ready to enter into serious negotiations about their future, were already setting to work to blame Britain for its unreasonable attitude. Commentators told the public that British protests were to be expected, but could be safely disregarded. The fact was that Security Council Resolution 502 was just not seen in Buenos Aires for what it was intended to be: a firm and clear denunciation of the invasion by the international community as a whole. It was seen merely as a move in the diplomatic game, which slowly became in Argentine minds more of a problem to Britain than to them.

The slow process of the erosion of Britain's diplomatic position, so well established at the outset, was to take just two months. On that first weekend of full-scale crisis, the Resolution came as almost the first real sign of hope in a situation that shook the foundations of the Government. Mrs Thatcher herself does not appear to have contemplated resignation. Lord Carrington offered her his on 3 April, and was pressed to withdraw it, but eventually on Monday 5 April, insisted, on the grounds that he had been responsible for foreign policy and that it was therefore he who should resign. With him went two junior ministers, Mr Atkins and Mr Luce. At the same time, as the first elements of the task force sailed from Portsmouth, where the job of loading them had gone on round the clock over the weekend, Mr Nott too placed his office at the Prime Minister's disposal. In a reply asking him to stay on in his post, Mrs Thatcher exonerated him from responsibility, since 'the Ministry of Defence is not the Department responsible for policy towards the Falkland Islands' and it was now vital that he should remain at his post in face of the 'possibility of armed action'.[38]

Simultaneously it was announced that Mr Pym had been appointed to succeed Lord Carrington as Foreign Secretary. An Etonian like his predecessor, Mr Pym had also won the Military Cross, in the Second World War serving as a Captain in the 9th Lancers.[39] After the war he had worked as a businessman in Liverpool, Birmingham and Hereford, before entering Parliament at a by-election in Cambridgeshire in 1961. His rise to ministerial office came through the Whip's Office to the crucial and delicate post of Secretary of State for Northern Ireland in 1973. It was interrupted by Mrs Thatcher's rise to the leadership but subsequently resumed with his appointment in 1978 as Opposition Spokesman on Foreign and Commonwealth Affairs. But it was Lord Carrington who was given the post itself in 1979, while Mr Pym took over the crucial management role of Leader of the House of Commons. In this position he had for some time been regarded as a potential successor to the Prime Minister herself, and now his inclusion in the Cabinet in one of its leading positions made his political position stronger than ever, a considerable asset to a harassed Government. For there was particular advantage to it in having the Secretary of State in the Commons, particularly one who was personally liked and had displayed his talents for promoting harmony between warring interests. It was indeed an irony that by the time he took over the post the principle of negotiating from strength had already been established, and the future outlines of the crisis, in which diplomacy would take a secondary role, were already clear.

4 Negotiating from strength

Many misperceptions about world politics stem from the simple fact that most people see the world in one analogy at a time. Most see it as a rectangular map. Thus, for example, in the United States the Western Hemisphere is seen as distinct from the rest of the world, and Argentina among other South American countries is seen as a neighbour of the United States. In fact the distance from New York to Buenos Aires is almost exactly the same as the distance from Southampton to Buenos Aires, and New York is nearer to London than it is to San Francisco. Some see the world as land and some as water, and if to some the sea divides, to others it acts as a link, as in the cases of Malaysia, Indonesia, and the Polynesian Islands. It is a purely land-centred view of our watery world that suggests that political links must necessarily follow land routes.

British commentators were quick to pick up the analogies between the Falklands and other islands they knew, such as the Hebrides, the Faeroes or even the Channel Islands. The instinct to defend them came easily. To fail to do so might suggest to other countries a dangerous lack of will to defend the British Isles themselves. Less easily came the further realisation of the distances involved, the fact that the Falklands were actually as far away from Britain as was Hawaii, and an assessment of the relative balance of land, air and sea involved in their strategic position. There was a general tendency to seize on one historical analogy and argue from that. The D-Day landings of the Second World War suggested that any frontal attack on the Argentine positions in the Falklands would be very difficult and might take months to prepare. Mr Healey emphasised the dangers of Argentine air power and the importance, indeed absolute necessity, of gaining strategic air supremacy, a theme subsequently pursued less reflectively by other MPs who perhaps knew less about the real strength of the Argentine air force. Conservatives tended to see President Galtieri as a latter-day Hitler and to assume that other nations would see him in the same light, and in both ways came perilously close to looking ridiculous.[1] For the very political strength of the Argentine military forces went hand in hand with a relatively small capacity for military action such as they had assumed in the invasion of the Falklands, though that is not to say that individuals, especially air force pilots, did not in the event fight with great skill and daring.

The strategic situation on Saturday 3 April was that the Argentine invasion had been successful, and hence all contingency plans based on the assumption of British control of the islands had to be discarded. British military action to repossess the islands was the new contingency, whether understood or not, for which the task force was formed. Even if, as the Government said, it was intended to exhibit it in such a way as to bring about a diplomatic settlement in advance of hostilities, it was only the clear evidence of willingness to use it that could make such a threat effective. For as far as Argentina was concerned Britain had nothing to give in negotiations. All it wanted was the islands, and those it now held. Possession is nine-tenths of the law.

Now although Argentina had a navy of its own, in practice little was known about the uses of naval power. The army was the dominant service, and inter-service rivalry was, as we have seen, an important part of the internal political fabric. Hence though some attention was paid in Buenos Aires to the sailing of the first elements of the task force, the light carriers *Hermes* and *Invincible*, on Monday 5 April none was given to the implications of a meeting of the British Privy Council at Windsor Castle the previous day. Yet it was at this meeting that an Order in Council was made empowering the Government to 'requisition for Her Majesty's service any British ship and anything on board such ship wherever the ship may be.'[2] From this Order began a process of requisitioning and chartering a fleet, ultimately of over sixty ships grossing more than 750,000 tons, to provide the essential services needed to move huge quantities of men and material to the South Atlantic, to keep them provisioned, and supplied with arms and ammunition, and to provide hospital and other facilities which would be needed in the event of armed conflict. The first to be taken over was the 45,000 ton P & O cruise liner *Canberra* as it passed Gibraltar on its way back to Southampton from a world cruise. The largest was to be the 67,000 ton flagship of the Cunard fleet, the *Queen Elizabeth II*, which sailed from Southampton on 12 May carrying an entire infantry brigade. The huge additional strength this represented, made possible only through the unusual size of the QE2, was to play a decisive part in reversing the odds in the battle for Port Stanley in June.

So, by an ancient but effective, simple device, the British Government was able to turn the capital ships of the Royal Naval task force and their attendant escorts into the spearhead of the largest amphibious operation attempted since the end of the Second World War. There was an irony that it was in dockyards threatened by closure and by men threatened with redundancy that the ships were made ready. But public support for the Government's action, soon to show itself even more unequivocally in the public opinion polls, was shown not least by the huge crowds that cheered the ships of all classes on their way, waving flags and showing as well as personal emotion a surge of patriotism such as has not been felt for many years. Interviewed on BBC television Mrs Thatcher put words to the feeling, which though sincerely meant and popular with her British audience won no support in the wider world of United Nations debates and anti-colonialism. 'We have to regain the Falklands for British sovereignty', she declared. 'It is still British and the people still wish to be British and owe their allegiance to the crown.'[3]

As the task force built up over a number of days, drawing vessels from a wide range of sources in Britain, the North Atlantic and the Mediterranean, its future shape and size gradually emerged. It was the carriers, one, the anti-submarine warfare/commando carrier *Hermes*, scheduled to be scrapped, and the other, the anti-submarine warfare carrier *Invincible*, already sold to the Australian government, that were the key to the whole operation. It was from their floating platforms that the Sea Harriers would have to fly to endeavour to place a temporary tactical air cover over any future operations. In theory at least, the Sea Harrier, despite its unique vertical take-off and landing capacity, would be no match for the high performance Argentine Mirages. But the missile batteries of the destroyer and frigate escorts, though they had never before been deployed in air-sea conflict on this scale, provided a different sort of protection against aerial attack, and would, it was hoped, prove at least adequate to protect the fleet itself.

Repossession of the islands would, however, involve the landing of troops. Argentine strategists calculated that even 5,000 men on the Falklands could defend it against a British attack of three times that number, but until the QE2 was chartered it appeared that the ratio would probably not reach 1 to 1. Worse still, the Argentines had chosen the ideal time of year to launch their invasion, just as winter was drawing on and temperatures in and around the islands were dropping back towards freezing point. Landing any number of troops in such conditions would not be easy. The key to doing it at all was the specially designed vessels, the *Fearless*, which sailed from Portsmouth on 6 April, and her consort the *Intrepid*, assault ships of some 12,000 tons, and the logistic landing ships *Sir Galahad* and *Sir Geraint*, of some 6,000 tons, which sailed the same day from Plymouth, loaded with 105 mm light guns, trucks and helicopters.[4]

The work of the helicopters would begin long before the fleet reached the South Atlantic, as they worked round the clock ferrying the supplies that had been so hastily loaded as ships became available to the places where they were to be used. The civilian vessels too had to be integrated into the overall plan. By the time *Canberra* docked on 7 April, preparations had already been made to fit her with a helicopter landing pad, a task that involved both the construction of a prefabricated steel platform and the design, with the aid of the original shipbuilders' plans, of supports and strengthening members to distribute the additional load safely. Once the fleet had passed Ascension Island the helicopters' role in looking out for submarine attack would become increasingly important, and would be continuous the whole time that the fleet was in the operational zone. In the operations themselves they would play a variety of roles; landing advance parties, speeding the landing itself with their lifting capability, ferrying troops and supplies rapidly across the boggy and inhospitable moorland of the Falklands themselves, and removing the wounded from the battle zone. To make sure that the most powerful heavy-lift helicopters available could be used in these ways when needed, the Government later chartered the huge Cunard container ship *Atlantic Conveyor*, which, loaded in addition with crated Sea Harrier and Air Force Harrier jet aircraft, could be used in effect as a third, 'do-it-yourself' aircraft carrier, and was in fact also used as an overnight 'parking lot' for Harriers.

A whole range of other ships were also necessary. First of all there were the ships of the Royal Fleet Auxilliary (RFA), specially designed for the long-range refuelling and supply of the fleet at sea.[5] It was the technique perfected by the Royal Navy, of refuelling at sea at speed while zigzagging to avoid attack, which provided endless fascination for Soviet observation vessels during the journey south, and which enabled it to deploy with the maximum rapidity. The auxiliaries themselves were replenished from chartered oil tankers. British Petroleum's *Tamar*, *Tay* and *Esk* were the first to be chosen. The requisitioning of Britain's largest sea-going tug, the *Salvageman*, and two others, the *Yorkshireman* and the *Irishman*, envisaged the possibility of the disablement of ships, while the conversion of the *Canberra* for the secondary role of hospital ship, and the requisitioning on 11 April of the schools' cruise ship *Uganda*, foresaw the necessity of medical treatment for wounded sailors, soldiers and marines. The *Uganda*, in port at Alexandria, cut short her cruise by three days, discharged her passengers at Naples, and sailed for Gibraltar, where enthusiastic workers facing the imminent closure of the British Royal Naval dockyard, or its transfer to private ownership, again worked with immense energy and enthusiasm to convert her for her new task. She sailed with her white paint and fresh red crosses still wet only minutes after welders had put the finishing touches to her helicopter flight deck. The North Sea vessel *Norland Ferry* was also called in to carry troops, while even smaller vessels were also commissioned to act as tenders and support vessels in inshore waters.

Though the ships came from many places and were of many kinds, they all converged on one point — Ascension Island, a lonely, volcanic island midway between the West Coast of Africa and Brazil. The island was under British sovereignty but dominated by the huge mid-Atlantic American air base from which the United States tracked all movement in the region. Regardless of its diplomatic stance, the United States was obliged, by the terms of its lease on the base, to give Britain full facilities there. Hence, while the fleet was assembling, Hercules C-130 transport aircraft were already beginning to arrive in increasing numbers, while a security blackout was imposed on all information about military movements. The unexpected arrival of the RFA *Fort Austin* on 6 April off the island, however, gave the first indication that the task force was on its way.[6] Thereafter its speed of movement would necessarily be limited by the speed of the slower vessels, along with the need to maintain a zone of protection around all of them.

Ascension, however, had considerable limitations as a forward base. Though 3,500 miles from Southampton, it was still some 3,500 miles from the Falklands and South Georgia. The value of its offshore anchorage was limited, and in any case the bulk of supplies had to be ferried in by air from the United Kingdom. With nowhere to land, on the other hand, the large transport aircraft would be of no use south of Ascension until and unless the Falklands themselves were repossessed. Though there were a number of possible military options in theory, therefore, only one stood out as an obvious choice: the so-called 'South Georgia option'.

The recapture of South Georgia had obvious diplomatic advantages. It was where the cause of conflict had arisen, and its capture would be a demonstration of British will to make its sovereignty effective. It had, and could have, only a small Argentine garrison, and its distance from the Falklands, let alone from Argentina itself, made it dependent on re-supply from sea and so placed the odds heavily in favour of the superior naval force. Its quick recapture therefore could be virtually guaranteed, and so represent the minimum use of force by Britain in conformity with the principles of Article 51 of the United Nations Charter. Such a demonstration in itself, some politicians argued, would put pressure on the Argentine Government to seek a diplomatic solution, before worse humiliation befell them in the Falklands themselves.

It also had military advantages. Though the sub-Antarctic climate was formidable enough, it was something that British troops had prepared for in NATO training in the north of Norway. By demonstrating this, the Argentines could be shown the capacity of British forces to resist the rigours of a Falkland winter. Much more important, however, was the fact that South Georgia would give the navy the inestimable boon of a safe and sheltered deep-water anchorage only 800 miles from the Falklands, which could give the troops some respite from the pounding of the South Atlantic seas, and which, thanks to the preparations of the past, was well enough equipped to allow substantial naval repairs to be undertaken in case of need.[7]

Its disadvantages were that it required a detachment of troops from the main task force which the force could not afford while the Falklands themselves were to be taken. It therefore involved an unavoidable delay which would give time for the Argentines further to reinforce their garrison and supplies on the Falklands themselves. It did not offer a satisfactory airstrip, though given time and machinery one could undoubtedly be constructed, and even if one were improvised, the Harriers with their limited range (even more limited if vertical take-off was used) would be unable to reach the Falklands from there. There were, on the other hand, no obvious diplomatic disadvantages. There was therefore no remaining obstacle to the adoption of the option save that it was so obvious that the Argentines must also have thought of it. Strategic surprise, therefore, could not be achieved, and it would have to be left to the task force commander, Rear Admiral John (Sandy) Woodward, to achieve tactical surprise as best he could.

Meanwhile there was one way in which almost immediate pressure could be brought to bear on the Argentines. It was known that at least one nuclear powered submarine, possibly more, could be in the area to pose an immediate threat to

naval resupply of the islands.[8] It was therefore possible for
Britain at once to indicate its determination to use this
weapon, to which Argentina had no effective counter, and so
at the least hamper the build-up of supplies and men on the
islands. On 7 April, therefore, formal warning was given in
London that with effect from 5.00 a.m. BST on Monday 12
April Britain would establish a maritime exclusion zone
(MEZ) within a 200 mile radius around the islands, and that
from that time any Argentine vessel sighted in the area was
liable to be sunk.[9]

This idea, which had first been suggested in Parliament by
Dr David Owen,[10] appeared to be wholly effective. By the
appointed time all vessels of the Argentine fleet had withdrawn to home waters. It was true that, including the period
of exercises beforehand, they had by then been at sea long
enough to have to refuel and resupply, but if so they made a
diplomatic virtue out of a necessity. For though the Junta
grandly countered the British proclamation by declaring a
similar zone not only round the islands, but also round South
Georgia and the South Sandwich Islands,[11] in practice it
would have been extremely foolish to have tried to enforce it.

The Haig Mission

The first period of diplomacy, up to 7 April, had been the
phase of immediate reaction to events. As far as Britain was
concerned, it had been very successful. Led by France and
Germany, countries of the Community had declared an arms
embargo against Argentina. The Commonwealth, too, had
displayed unity in condemning the Argentine aggression. New
Zealand had joined Britain in severing diplomatic relations;
Canada and Australia had withdrawn their Ambassadors from
Buenos Aires. The United Nations Security Council had
passed Resolution 502. Mr Pym was therefore able to face
the House of Commons in his new role as Foreign Secretary
with a brisk confidence, and to receive great applause for his
confident assertion: 'Britain does not appease dictators'.[12]
His triumph was the greater for the fact that his Labour
opponent, Mr Healey, badly misjudged the mood of the
occasion, alternately challenging Mrs Thatcher to resign and
lecturing her on the 'appallingly difficult and dangerous

situation to which the Government has exposed the nation'.
It almost seemed that he was more interested in defeating the
Government than defeating the Argentines. Yet — 'Nevertheless we shall,' he said, 'support the Government's efforts to
solve this crisis so long as we are satisfied that their activities
are inspired by the desire for a diplomatic solution consistent
with the wishes of the Falkland Islanders and the principles
of the United Nations and that their actions are well calculated
to fulfil those principles.'[13]

The second period of diplomacy, which commenced with
that debate, was the search for a mediated solution. The
period in turn can be subdivided into three phases: the Haig
mission, the Peruvian plan, and the Secretary General's good
offices. Crucial to the beginning of it were two things:
Argentina's failure to gain expected diplomatic support, and
the 'even handed' approach of the United States.

Though the United States Administration had initially
condemned the invasion and had voted for Resolution 502,
it had been careful to avoid outright alignment with either
side. Hints were dropped that Secretary of State Alexander
Haig was available as a mediator, and, following a meeting
between him and Dr Costa Méndez, it was formally announced
from the White House that President Reagan had commissioned him to visit both London and Buenos Aires in the
search for peace.[14] Dr Costa Méndez was of course not only
interested in presenting the appearance of being a reasonable
man, prepared to negotiate. He had also just come from a
meeting of the Non-aligned countries in New York, where he
had a lukewarm reception. Four countries spoke in favour
of the Argentine claims: Peru, Panama, Ecuador and Nicaragua.
None supported the act of invasion, and all appealed to both
sides to begin negotiations.[15] The fact that Dr Costa Méndez
had long been a public opponent of Argentine membership
of the Non-aligned movement undoubtedly helped to
explain the delegates' lack of enthusiasm, but the fact remained that Argentina had as yet little real support, and
could not afford to offend the powerful President of the
United States. Even among the Latin American countries,
the overwhelming majority of whom had long supported
Argentine claims in principle, translating this support into

action was going to be very difficult so long as the United
States remained uncommitted.

Al Haig had the obvious attraction as a mediator of being
personally acceptable to both sides. His background had been
entirely military, until first Henry Kissinger and then Presi
dent Nixon had brought him in to a key position within the
White House Staff of which he soon became Chief. In Nixon's
last days it had been he who had kept the wheels of govern
ment turning, and engineered the transfer of power from
Nixon to Ford; a delicate task that might have tried the
diplomatic skills of the most accomplished professional
administrator.[16] His reward had been appointment to the
post of Supreme Allied Commander in Europe. Through
his NATO responsibilities he was well known in London
where it appeared that he was widely respected and liked
while at the same time his military background ensured him a
reception in Buenos Aires that no civilian could have obtained
In any case as President Reagan's Secretary of State he held
a position of great significance to both parties, both allies of
the United States: Britain through NATO and Argentina
through the Rio Pact. His only disadvantage, on the other
hand, was a talent for longwinded and complex sentences
which had among American newsmen given rise to the self
explanatory phrase 'Haigspeak', describing a statement which
was long, obscure and possibly wrong. A diplomat must have
the ability to mislead others. He must not in any circumstances mislead himself.

Within hours of the President's announcement on 7 April
the Secretary of State had left for London, where he arrived
the next afternoon. It had already been made clear to him in
advance that Britain would not negotiate until the Argentines
had left the islands, and that Britain wished the islanders to
be restored to British administration. In talks with Mr Pym
at the Foreign Office, this position was reaffirmed, while
Haig for his part explored a variety of possibilities both
for temporary and long-term arrangements, including the
'lease-back' proposal. Further discussions ensued over a
working dinner at No 10 Downing Street, with Mrs Thatcher
Mr Pym and senior officials.[17]

The following day, 9 April, was Good Friday. The Secretary

spent it in transit to Buenos Aires in his specially equipped white United States Airforce jet, while Dr Costa Méndez, who had returned from Washington direct, said in Buenos Aires that he believed the danger of war was receding. President Galtieri, on the other hand, asked whether Argentina was going to fight, said simply 'That is what we are going to do.'[18] In an artistic touch, the Junta allowed the streets of the capital on Saturday to be filled with a vast crowd, estimated at some 200,000, demonstrating in favour of its policy on the Malvinas. The bulk of the demonstrators had been rallied by the peronista labour unions, only too grateful to have a chance to win the Government's favour for their own future legalisation, and as General Haig's car inched its way through the crowds, they set to work with a will to show how united they were against any hint of a sell-out.[19]

The Secretary held separate talks with the Foreign Minister and with the President, who allowed himself the apparently more optimistic statement that 'there is always the possibility of a solution while talks are going on'.[20] Then, after a further round of talks on Easter Sunday, Haig left again for London, taking with him what he termed 'specific ideas for discussion'. These ideas appear to have included four main points. An Argentine withdrawal from the islands would be made at the same time as the British task force returned to Britain. The Argentine flag would continue to fly on the islands. The islanders would be allowed to choose their own form of government. While a permanent solution was being worked out, instead of troops, Argentine police would be deployed on the islands.[21]

Discussions of these points resumed in London on 12 April just after the British MEZ had come into effect, and went on for eleven hours. Taking part, in addition to General Haig, were, among others, Mr Thomas Enders, Assistant Secretary of State for Inter-American Affairs and General Vernon Walters, who had already visited Argentina several months previously as special envoy of President Reagan, at which time he had been trying to enlist Argentine support for United States policy in Central America, and on the British side, the Foreign and Defence Secretaries, as well as the Prime Minister herself. It was made quite clear to the Secretary that none of the Argentine proposals were acceptable as they stood, and for his part General Haig appeared to believe that the future of Mrs Thatcher as Prime Minister might be endangered if concessions on such a scale were required of her. In eleven hours of intensive discussions, details of British counter-proposals were worked out.[22] While still insisting on Argentine withdrawal as essential to all further discussion, these now envisaged, instead of a return of the islands to British administration (and a purely nominal period had at one time been considered), the establishment of a tripartite administration by Britain, Argentina and the United States. But when this proposal was put by telephone by General Haig to Dr Costa Méndez in Buenos Aires it was rejected. The Secretary prepared to return to Buenos Aires that night.

His baggage was already on the aircraft when a further message caused him to change his mind and to stay in London overnight for further talks on the morning of 13 April. Late in the afternoon, after a further round of telephone calls, and a brief visit by the Foreign Secretary to his suite in the Churchill Hotel, he finally departed, but for Washington and not for Buenos Aires.[23] Stating that the situation was 'still dangerous and increasingly so',[24] he indicated that he wished to report to President Reagan before continuing his efforts to secure peace.

While Haig was in Washington the British Parliament was recalled from its Easter recess to hold a special debate on the situation on Wednesday 14 April. In her opening statement Mrs Thatcher made it clear that the proposal made by Argentina on the Monday night (12 April) could not possibly have been accepted, but that the situation seemed to have improved somewhat on Tuesday. Mr Haig's next meetings in Buenos Aires would, however, be 'crucial' if peace were to be secured. If the maritime exclusion zone were breached Britain would take it as the clearest possible sign that the Junta had abandoned the search for peace. In order to ensure that the strongest possible naval, military and air presence could be maintained in the South Atlantic the British Government was prepared to commit its forces for an extended period and at whatever cost might be required. Commissioning the assault ship HMS *Intrepid* would double the amphibious capacity of the task force, and requisitioning the *Atlantic Conveyor* would double the number of Harrier aircraft that could be deployed in the area. The wishes of the Falkland Islanders must be paramount and they must be able freely to determine their own future. This they could not do until the Argentines had left the islands. The Government was ready to resort to force in self defence until they had done so.[25]

There was again a rare and remarkable degree of unity in the speeches that followed in supporting the Government's actions thus far. Though Labour spokesmen were clearly unhappy about the possibility that force might have to be used, they did not argue for concessions, and Mr Healey, as did other speakers, indicated that in his opinion Britain was entitled to ask for a direct commitment, and not merely mediation, from the United States. Such comments could in fact only increase the embarrassment already felt in Washington about the reports from ABC-TV that the United States was in any case already supplying Britain with intelligence, including satellite photographs and weather reports for the Falklands area. It was also stated, with less certainty, that the Soviet Union, which by 8 April had moved to support Argentina, was helping its Government with satellite information and intercepts of British radio transmissions. Certainly task force vessels were reporting keen interest by Soviet AGI intelligence gathering vessels in every aspects of their preparation for battle, and the RN guard ship HMS *Leeds Castle* had to ensure that one particularly persistent one was kept as far away as possible from Ascension Island.[26]

The British Government's diplomatic position abroad had meanwhile continued to strengthen. Most dramatic, because most unexpected, was the decision of the Foreign Ministers of the Community to impose a ban on imports from Argentina for an initial period of four weeks.[27] The decision, which was unanimous, had been taken with quite unaccustomed speed and decisiveness, even while the long-unresolved debate about Britain's contribution to the Community was coming to a vote. But at the same time, after two inconclusive attempts in four days to get together for an emergency session, the Organisation of American States in its first meeting of the crisis, behind closed doors in Washington, showed that support for Argentina in its ranks was by no means the foregone conclusion that many had expected.[28] Meanwhile the worsening situation in Argentina's already overtaxed financial situation was making it evidently vulnerable to economic pressure, especially if that of the Community and Commonwealth were to be reinforced with that of the United States. In the course of the week, at any rate, statements from Argentina became noticeably more encouraging, only to harden again with a declaration by President Galtieri himself that Argentine sovereignty in the Falklands was 'unrenounceable'.[29]

The second round of the Haig Mission began on the evening of 15 April with a telephone call from President Galtieri to President Reagan in which President Galtieri said that he was prepared to comply with United Nations Resolution 502 and to withdraw Argentine forces from the islands if the British task force was also withdrawn. President Reagan, in reply, called for 'flexibility and restraint by all parties.'[30] The call coincided with the arrival in Buenos Aires of General Haig, who, despite his sympathy with Britain, had already been reported to have been as impatient with Britain's intransigence as with that of Argentina. In addition he had been under strong pressure from the 'Latin Americanists' in the State Department to avert a conflict, and the most conspicuous of these was none other than Mrs Jeane Kirkpatrick, the American Ambassador to the United Nations, who had dined the night after the attack at the Argentine Embassy and subsequently with the Argentine delegation to the United Nations, had denied that the Argentine attack necessarily constituted armed aggression, and made no secret of her belief that the conflict threatened United States relations, not just with Argentina, but with the whole of Latin America.[31] One of the most outspoken countries in support of Argentina was Venezuela. Although a democratic country, with no ideological affinity between its government and that of Argentina, Venezuela had greeted the independence of its neighbour Guayana (former British Guiana) with a claim to some two-thirds of its territory, and that claim, it had already indicated, it was not prepared to 'freeze' any longer when the current treaty expired in July. Hence General Haig, on his way south, had already called at Caracas to talk to Venezuelan leaders.[32]

In five hours of talks on 16 April, the Secretary of State got nowhere. Dr Costa Méndez had been astonished by the British response to the invasion, and having totally failed to predict it, had derided it. 'The English reaction is so absurd, so disproportionate', he had said. 'This seems like a chapter in a science fiction novel.'[33] Asked what he thought about Mrs Thatcher, he said: 'Not a lot. I would love to tell you but you could not print it.'[34] He expressed optimism about the talks, because Mr Haig had said 'that he had some novel ideas and that the British stand had changed'. But when confronted by the hint from the Secretary that in the event of failure to agree the United States might have to side with Britain, he still gave no significant ground. Indeed, in an obviously derisory gesture, he offered Britain sovereignty over South Georgia — a move which abundantly explains the Argentine reason both for claiming and for invading the island in the first place.[35]

General Haig's urgent desire to find a solution was confirmed by the intensity with which he now pursued it, his large black car shuttling between his hotel, the Foreign Ministry and the Casa Rosada, where on 17 April he met all three members of the Junta. On Sunday 18 April, he met the Foreign Minister in the morning, and the President in the afternoon, after the Argentines had the previous night asked him to postpone his departure to hold further meetings, and talks went on for some twelve hours, before the Secretary returned to his hotel at 2.00 a.m. on the 19th, gloomy about the prospects of success.[36] Only half an hour later, however, he again received a telephone call which brought renewed hope of concessions, and at a meeting in the morning at the presidential palace, the Secretary was given what he termed 'significant' counter-proposals.[37] Meanwhile the Argentine fleet, which had been said to be ready to sail from Puerto Belgrano on the previous Friday, remained close to shore and made no attempt to challenge the blockade of the Falklands.[38] Stating that his work in Buenos Aires was now finished, Haig left for Washington, while the results of his discussions were communicated to the British Government 'I am more convinced than ever that war in the South Atlantic would be the greatest of tragedies,' he told reporters, 'and that time is running out.'[39]

The Argentine counterproposals included four main points. Troops would be withdrawn on both sides to their normal places of operation, which meant, in the Argentine case Argentina, and in the British case the United Kingdom. An interim adminstration by a council of an equal number of British and Argentine islanders would be established. The United Nations would supervise the transition, which would end on 31 December 1982. Meanwhile Argentines would have rights to buy land and to settle on the islands.[40]

Such proposals were intended to lead to eventual Argentine sovereignty over the islands, and in the nature of things, had they been accepted, they could hardly have had any other effect. It was a measure of the British Government's determination to try to reach a negotiated settlement, and to aid Mr Haig's efforts, that they did not disclose their terms. Questioned in the House of Commons on Tuesday 20 April, Mrs Thatcher said bluntly: 'Of course we shall try to seek a diplomatic solution, but we have to be true to our objectives. I cannot disguise from the House that the Argentine proposals at present before us fall short, in some important respects, of the objectives and of the requirements as expressed in this House.'[41]

Questioned by Mr Foot, the Prime Minister indicated that the proposals were Argentine ones, and not those of Mr Haig himself. 'We regard this as a stage in the negotiating process which must now be continued', she said. Mr Pym would therefore be visiting Washington on Thursday 22 April, to follow up the proposals. But she would not disclose details, going only so far as to say: 'Among the many problems presented by the Argentine proposals is that they fail to provide that the Falkland Islanders should be able to determine their own destiny. The House has always said that the wishes of the islanders are paramount.'

In response to one member who voiced a general distaste for the idea that Argentine police should be brought on to the islands, she pointed out that before the invasion there were in fact only two policemen on the islands: 'it was a very law-abiding place'.[42]

Further evidence of the contents of the proposals came from the Junta in Buenos Aires in a communiqué at 1.00 a.m. on 21 April, which declared: 'We have given guarantees and assurances that the opportunity exists for a limited period of transition in such a way that afterwards the ultimate result can be nothing less than the speedy exercise of our sovereignty over the Malvinas islands.'[43]

This communiqué merely restated in public what the British Cabinet had already been told in private, namely that there was and could be no concession on the Argentine side on the issue of sovereignty. In reply Mr Pym made it clear in the House of Commons that though he hoped that the negotiations might still be successful, the point at issue was 'continuing efforts by Argentina to establish by her aggression and by defiance of the UN — a defiance continued and aggravated by her reinforcement of her invasion forces — what could not be established by peaceful means.'

The issue here is one of international order. We are dealing with the basic charter of the United Nations, of which self-determination forms a part. It is a wide issue which has associations and connotations for many countries and peoples not just, as in this case, the wishes of the islanders. Therefore, that is an important issue. The Government has made their position clear on all those central issues.[44]

At the end of the questioning, in reply to Mr Richard Douglas (Lab — Dunfermline), the Foreign Secretary ruled out the possibility of military action so long as negotiations were 'in play'. A few minutes later, he returned to the House, and most unusually, made it quite clear that this was not what he had intended to say. 'The whole thrust of my answers throughout the exchanges was to indicate I was using every endeavour — which indeed I am — to achieve a peaceful settlement but that, however regrettable, the use of force could not be ruled out.'[45] So that the point could not be missed, the Prime Minister herself repeated it twice to MPs in the House at question time on Thursday 22 April.[46] The following day, while Britain notified Argentina through the Swiss Embassy that any close approach to units of the task force by Argentine vessels would be treated as an act of war,[47] Admiral Woodward indicated that it was his intention to establish an air as well as a sea blockade of the Falklands at the earliest possible opportunity.[48] Meanwhile in both Britain and Argentina last minute checks were made on the readiness of the forces. Mrs Thatcher paid a two-hour visit to the Royal Navy's operational headquarters at Northwood, in the north-west of London, and lunched with the Commander in Chief of the Fleet, Admiral Sir John Fieldhouse, and his staff before going off to Chequers, the Prime Minister's official country residence, for the weekend.[49] And President Galtieri paid his first visit to the Falklands on the Thursday to review his troops, staying overnight, and returning by way of Southern Argentine ports and military installations to Buenos Aires. He said:

I am convinced that the blue and white flag of Argentina will never come down from the Malvinas. We really want a peaceful settlement. . . . We have warm hearts but what is needed now is cool heads. The British may defeat us; but they cannot break our spirits. Our material things may be destroyed but our spirits cannot be broken.[50]

The recapture of South Georgia

Despite all the pointers that the move was on its way, the recapture of South Georgia by British forces on Sunday 25 April, was achieved with almost complete tactical surprise, and with no British casualties. What was not generally known for some weeks afterwards was that this was not only due to good planning, but to luck which, having first seemed adverse, at the last minute gave the landing forces an unexpected bonus.

The attack had in fact begun on the night of 21 April, when fifteen men of the Special Air Service Regiment (SAS) were landed by helicopter on the Fortuna glacier, overlooking the Argentine garrison at Grytviken. In windspeeds of over 100 mph (180 kph) and sub-zero temperatures, they were unable to stay there and were withdrawn with the loss of two helicopters. Eventually a successful landing was made from rubber boats on Grass Island, from which the men were able to report back that the Argentine garrison was idle and careless. But it was sheer good luck that task force helicopters landing reconnaissance patrols to the north of Grytviken on Sunday morning sighted and attacked the Argentine ex-US Guppy class submarine *Santa Fe* as it made for the harbour.[51] The submarine, on fire and leaking oil, beached in the harbour. Before its sixty crew and reinforcements for the garrison had time to orientate themselves, the landing had been brought forward, and by 5.45 p.m. the white flag was run up by the Argentine garrison. A detachment at Leith, which refused to accept the surrender by the Argentine Commander Major Carlos Astiz, was taken the next day without casualties. In all, 156 military and thirty-eight civilian prisoners were taken, a total much exceeding the number of British marines involved.[52]

This action transformed the situation. From a military point of view the capture of a secure forward base was of inestimable value, as we have already seen. From a diplomatic point of view, however, the consequences were unfortunate. In the course of the long journey South of the task force, even some British MPs had had time to forget that it was the armed invasion by Argentina of the Falklands that had led to the creation of the task force. They had come to speak urgently of the necessity of not 'firing the first shot'. In the United States, Senators and Representatives who had met Mr Pym were fully aware of the causes of the dispute, and had already been urging on the Administration open support for the British side. But the State Department had maintained the view that 'the United States will not automatically abandon its honest broker role even if fighting starts', and Mr Pym, questioned whether a South Georgia operation was imminent, had been at some pains to spread confusion on that score. News of the incident now came as Mr Pym had left Washington, and Dr Costa Méndez had arrived there to attend the Special Meeting of the Organisation of American States scheduled at his request for Monday 26 April.

This gave Dr Costa Méndez an opportunity to appeal to world opinion that he was hardly likely to miss. He had already let it be known that he was coming to Washington with ideas for 'a possible way out', which he wished to discuss with Mr Haig. Now, as he hobbled, grim-faced, across the airport in New York, he told waiting reporters that his country was 'now technically in a state of war' with Britain.[53] His purpose, and that of the majority that had supported his call for a meeting of the OAS, was to call for collective action against Britain. But among the thirty countries represented at the meeting, twenty-one, including both Argentina and the United States, were also signatories of the Rio Pact of 1947 and Argentina had already indicated its intention in advance of the meeting of invoking Article 6 of that Treaty, branding Britain as an aggressor. For this purpose, the taking of South Georgia could hardly have come at a better time. Indeed it might even give Dr Costa Méndez the pretext to invoke Article 3 of the Treaty, binding the signatories to give armed assistance in the event of an attack from outside the hemisphere on any one of them.

Of course the framers of the Treaty had not envisaged the possibility that an American state would make a deliberate attack on a country outside the hemisphere and then try to shield itself behind the Treaty. Back in 1947, they had been primarily concerned with an attack by the Soviet Union, which they thought by definition would be unprovoked. Moreover the Latin American States had always resisted any attempt, whether from the United States or elsewhere, to extend the provisions of the treaty, say to internal subversion, and it did not apply in the event of an attack by one American state upon another. Given that Argentina was claiming that the Falklands were in effect an American state territory, and hence their original attack was not an attack, the British counterattack ought logically not to have been a counterattack. However, in such matters, emotion, not reason, rules.

Like the Treaty, the Organization of American States owed its origin to the work of the United States. It was, however, not a defence organisation as such, but a regional association within the United Nations, and over the years the United States had been able to use its skill in parliamentary management to obtain from its meetings a series of resolutions favourable to its position within the hemisphere.[54] It was the OAS that decided to exclude Cuba and to impose a ban on trade with that country after the Cuban

Missile Crisis of 1962. It was in the OAS, too, though by a bare majority, that the United States had obtained support for its unilateral intervention in the Dominican Republic in 1965.[55] However in the 1970s the Organization, which had its headquarters in Washington, had become increasingly restive at its role as a virtual extension of the State Department, and a series of attempts had been made to set up rival groupings, while the Carter Administration's support for moves to condemn human rights violations had brought threats not only from Argentina but from other states with military regimes to leave it. Consequently in 1982 its delegates were not in a mood to take any lead from the United States that cut across what they regarded as an issue of the independence of the hemisphere from outside interference.

There were, besides, other less admirable pressures at work.

Venezuela's claim to Guayanese territory has already been mentioned. But many other countries had territorial disputes with their neighbours. Of these the most significant was Peru. Peru, after twelve years of military rule, had returned to civilian government in 1980. It had a long-standing distrust of Chile, with which Argentina had been virtually at war, and so in any case was angling for Argentine support. But in addition it had a long-standing dispute over the possession of the frontier region on the Marañon River, a tributary of the Amazon, with its neighbour Ecuador. The dispute had led to war and been resolved in Peru's favour in 1942, in the middle of the Second World War, but the settlement had never been accepted by Ecuador, and in February 1981 the forces of the two countries had clashed in armed conflict in the Condor Mountains.[56] Within days of the Argentine occupation of the Falklands, the Peruvian Minister of Defence, who was a soldier in a civilian Cabinet, had expressed strong support for the Argentine position. General Cisneros had spent his cadet days at the Argentine Military Academy and had acquired the nickname 'El Gaucho'. His Prime Minister, Sr Manuel Ulloa, had spent much of the 1970s in exile in Buenos Aires, and was a frequent companion in its night clubs of Dr Costa Méndez.[57]

The revolutionary government of Nicaragua, the most left wing government in the OAS (since Cuba was excluded), might have seemed an even less likely ally for a regime with undoubted affinities with the one they themselves had overthrown in 1979. But Nicaragua had claims on a group of islands in the Caribbean, the San Andrés and Providencia Archipelago, which in 1929 had been awarded to Colombia. At the first hint that they wished to revive those claims, President Turbay Ayala of Colombia had rushed troop reinforcements to the islands, but Nicaragua was now a strong and vocal supporter of Argentina and led the pressure for a strong resolution condemning Britain.[58]

The final resolution did not actually call for armed support for Argentina, since Dr Costa Méndez, aware that he could not obtain the necessary fourteen votes in the meeting for such a move, wisely did not ask for it.[59] But what he got — a resolution surprisingly described in Britain as 'moderate' — contained two points of the greatest value to his case, and marked, in fact, the first marked shift of support away from Britain as the aggrieved party.[60]

First of all, the resolution began with a clear condemnation of Britain, the ministers having resolved in paragraph one: 'To urge the Government of Great Britain and Northern Ireland to cease immediately the hostilities it is carrying on within the security region established by Article 4 of the Inter-American Treaty of Reciprocal Assistance and to refrain from any act that could affect inter-American peace and security.'

Argentina, on the other hand, was only asked 'to refrain from taking any action that might exacerbate the situation'.

Secondly, the resolution then proceeded to urge both parties 'to call an immediate truce that will make it possible to resume and develop normally the negotiations aimed at a peaceful settlement of the conflict, bearing in mind *the rights of sovereignty of the Republic of Argentina over the Falklands* and the interests of the islanders [my italics].'

Among other provisions, moreover, the resolution contained a specific clause deploring 'the adoption of members of the European Economic Community and other states of coercive measures of an economic and political nature which are prejudicial to the Argentine nation', since they were not covered by Resolution 502 of the Security Council.

This was the only reference to Resolution 502 in the entire resolution and constituted nothing less than a complete reversal of its intended effect, though since the OAS was a regional organisation, no resolution on its part could override a Security Council resolution.

Mr Haig, who had been given a frosty reception by delegates on Monday, when he blamed Argentina for being the first to use force, and said that the dispute should not be handled within the collective security framework of the Rio Treaty, had by this action virtually terminated his mission, and he received no thanks from the delegates for it. Argentine news agencies, who were trying to maintain that Argentine forces were still fighting in 'the interior' of South Georgia (a geographical absurdity), were swift to indicate that the idea that the mission should continue had been virtually rejected. However Mr Haig had in fact met Dr Costa Méndez directly on several occasions during the meeting, and having failed to get each side to accept the proposals of the other, had now advanced his own proposals, which had been communicated to both sides. Since the United States had, along with Chile, Colombia and Trinidad and Tobago, abstained on the final OAS resolution, it appeared that the peace effort was still in being, even if by general agreement it had reached a critical stage.[61]

Tightening the screw

If the Haig Mission was in trouble, however, there was no real alternative in sight. Earlier the Peruvians had offered their services and made rather general suggestions for peaceful negotiations.[62] But after the vote at the OAS, when Peru was among the seventeen votes cast for a resolution that was hardly favourable to Britain, its President was unlikely to be an acceptable mediator as far as London was concerned. It was an unfortunate, though not necessarily disastrous coincidence, that the obvious person to take Mr Haig's place, the Secretary General of the United Nations, Sr Javier Pérez de Cuellar, was also Peruvian, and in fact a former Foreign Minister of that country. Following the South Georgia landing, the Secretary General had issued a press statement, which merely called on both parties to observe Resolution 502 and to refrain from any action that would broaden the conflict.'[63] There was considerable dissension between Mr Foot and Mrs Thatcher in a rowdy exchange in the House of Commons in London on 27 April as to how this statement should be interpreted, but Mrs Thatcher insisted on her view that as long as Argentina was in breach of Resolution 502 military operations must continue, or the lives of British troops would be unnecessarily at risk.[64]

What the Government had decided upon, however, was not the sudden attack on the Falklands themselves predicted rather wildly in some quarters, but a gradual and careful tightening of the screw on the occupying forces. On 29 April the Government therefore proclaimed that with effect from 11.00 a.m. GMT on the following day, 30 April, British forces would establish a Total Exclusion Zone (TEZ) round the islands, and that it would apply to all ships and all aircraft of any country aiding the illegal occupation of the islands, whether in the sea or air, or in the case of aircraft on the ground at the airport at Port Stanley, unless they had authority from the Ministry of Defence in London. Like the MEZ before it, it covered a radius of 200 nautical miles from latitude 51° 40' south and longitude 59° 39' west.[65] In addition, it will be remembered, Britain had already given notice that any Argentine vessels approaching vessels of the task force would be treated as hostile, regardless of the position of the ships concerned.

'Gentle persuasion', Mrs Thatcher said in the House of Commons on 29 April, opening the second emergency debate in a week, 'will not make the Argentine Government give up what they have seized by force. Our military response to the situation has been measured and controlled.'[66]

The 'official American proposals' of Mr Haig had been communicated to both sides. They had not been made public and it was for him to make them public at the appropriate time. But the proposals were 'complex and difficult' and inevitably they bore 'all the hallmarks of compromise in both their substance and language'. The conflict could be ended by immediate Argentine withdrawal, and Britain would then be prepared to enter into negotiations 'with a view to solving the underlying dispute.' Britain, as the aggrieved party, could not forfeit its right of self-defence under the Charter of the United Nations. The United Nations in itself did not have power to enforce its decisions, but the Government was in daily contact with the Secretary General, who had already indicated that he would take no initiative until adequate groundwork had been laid, it was clear that his action had the support of both sides, and he had a clear mandate to act from the Security Council.[67]

In fact within twenty-four hours the package of proposals was public, because it was not accepted by the Argentine Government.

It involves: . . . a cessation of hostility; withdrawal of both Argentine and British forces; termination of sanctions; establishment of a United States–United Kingdom–Argentine interim authority to maintain the agreement; continuation of the traditional local administration with Argentine participation; procedures for encouraging cooperation in the development of the islands; and a framework for negotiation on final settlement, taking into account the wishes of both sides and the wishes of the inhabitants.[68]

The news that it had not been accepted was announced in Washington by Mr Haig on the morning of 30 April, following a meeting of the National Security Council, and at the same time as he announced United States support for Britain and limited economic sanctions on Argentina. Dr Costa Méndez protested: 'We have made observations, but that does not mean that we have rejected the plan.'[69] Nevertheless in stating, after a half-hour interview with the Secretary General, that Argentina was 'ready to discuss every aspect of the problem, except Argentine sovereignty over the islands' he underlined the crucial importance of what Mr Haig had earlier said in his public statement:

Argentina's position remains that it must receive an assurance now of eventual sovereignty or an immediate *de facto* role in governing the islands which would lead to sovereignty.
For its part, the British Government has continued to affirm the need to respect the views of the inhabitants in any settlement.
The United States has thus far refrained from adopting measures in response to the seizure of the islands that could have interfered with our ability to work with both sides in the search for peace.

The British Government has shown complete understanding for this position. Now, however, in the light of Argentina's failure to accept a compromise, we must take steps to underscore that the United States cannot and will not condone the use of unlawful force to resolve disputes.[70]

It was the United States, therefore, that decided that Argentina was not prepared to reach a compromise. This was fortunate, for it saved the British Government from the embarrassment, if not worse, of having either to accept or to reject terms that would have fallen far short of its original stated objectives. The fact is, that in any negotiation it is always easier for a mediator to secure concessions from the party willing to concede them, regardless of the justice of its case or the cause of the dispute. A posture of complete intransigence in such circumstances can win undeserved success. The British Government had under Haig's pressure been prepared to concede a tripartite administration, rather than a return to British rule. They might have accepted the compromise given that it had the authority of the United States. But they still did not trust Argentine intentions, and the collapse of the negotiations therefore freed them from the burden of any compromises proposed so far. Or so it seemed. Mr Haig had, however, concluded his statement with a warning, and the warning was addressed to Britain as much as Argentina. 'The United States remains ready to assist the parties in finding that settlement. A strictly military outcome cannot endure over time. In the end there will have to be a negotiated settlement acceptable to the interested parties. Otherwise, we will all face unending hostility and insecurity in the South Atlantic.'[71]

But at 4.40 a.m. the next day, Saturday 1 May, the screw was tightened further, and the armed conflict for the repossession of the Falklands themselves had begun.[72]

TABLE 3: Balance of power in the South Atlantic at 21 May 1982

ARGENTINA	BRITAIN	
Air		
14 Skyhawk bombers	1 Vulcan bomber	
6 Tracker S-2a anti-submarine		
11 Canberra bombers		
68 Skyhawk ground-attack	40 Sea Harriers	
26 Dagger interceptors		
18 Mirage III interceptors		
45 Pucara counterinsurgency		
10 Neptune maritime patrol		
3 Super-Etendard interceptors		
Sea		
1 aircraft carrier	2 anti-submarine warfare carriers	
	1 guided missile destroyer (County Class)	
	1 guided missile destroyer (Type 82)	
2 guided missile destroyers (Type 42)	2 guided missile destroyers (Type 42)	
9 frigates	4 frigates (Type 21)	
	2 frigates (Type 22)	
	2 frigates (Type 12)	
	2 assault ships	
3 diesel submarines	—	
—	?2 nuclear-powered submarines	
Land		
10,500 soldiers and marines on Falklands	3,500 marines	awaiting landing at Port San Carlos
	2,500 soldiers	
130,000 soldiers in Argentina	3,500 soldiers	on QE2 off South Georgia

Source: *The Times*, 3 May 1982, as amended by later information.

5 Negotiating the non-negotiable

Enforcing the blockade

The attack on the airfield at Port Stanley marked the end of one phase in the crisis and the opening of a new one. But it did not, as was widely believed in both Britain and Argentina, mean the end of diplomacy and the beginning of conflict. The military actions of the conflict were designed to secure diplomatic ends. How far they did so, and what other consequences they had, will be the theme of this chapter.

In military terms, the attack was well planned and apparently very successful. An RAF Vulcan bomber, specially converted for the purpose, had flown from Ascension Island, and flew back again on a round trip of some 8,000 miles, refuelling in mid-air five times on the way, to drop twenty-one 1,000 lb bombs along the main runway. Then a wave of Sea Harriers from HMS *Hermes*, ninety miles off shore, flew low across the airfield, each with three more bombs, to ensure that the runway was cratered and inoperative. All returned safely, and reported that the attack had been effective: the runway cratered, stores of fuel and ammunition destroyed or on fire, and military installations on the airfield destroyed.[1]

The attack was a logical and necessary step if the islands were to be cut off from resupply from Argentina, and it represented the minimum amount of force necessary to achieve that aim. To be on the safe side it had been coupled with a Harrier attack on the grass airstrip at Goose Green, and in the further course of the campaign it was followed up at regular intervals by further raids and naval bombardment designed to stop the Argentine garrison from using heavy earthmoving equipment to fill up the craters. Reports from the Argentines that these attacks had had no significant effect on their capacity to resupply the garrison at Port Stanley were confidently discounted throughout the campaign, as just one more of the many wild boasts coming from Buenos Aires.[2] British reporters who entered Port Stanley after its fall, therefore, were as surprised as anyone to learn from the local inhabitants that, not only had the Argentine Hercules transports been able to keep up their flights throughout the period, but indeed the last one had left only the previous day, laden with Argentine officials, newsmen and television reporters who had been living it up at their Government's expense. Given the contrast with their own conditions, the British reporters were not particularly pleased.[3]

In the first few days, however, there was no particular reason to doubt that the blockade would be effective, nor that the Argentines would try very hard to breach, and if possible break it. President Galtieri made no secret of his intentions in a speech to the nation on the evening of 1 May, in which, taking full advantage of the international connotations of the day, he sought to portray Argentina as a peaceloving nation struggling against British colonialism, backed by the treachery of the United States, supported only on its side by the 'solidarity and fraternity' of the other American states and 'the understanding and the support' of the non-aligned. 'Now the British empire, emboldened by the supposed results of its campaign of pressure, is resorting to the direct and overt use of force', he said. 'There remains no other recourse but to respond with military action to this violence.'[4]

President Galtieri's argument in support of his view that in invading the islands Argentina had in fact supported rather than refuted its claim to be acting in a peaceable manner, is both interesting and significant. 'Attempts have been made to portray us as bloody aggressors when the truth, as everyone knows, is that in recovering unredeemed territory we prefer to die than kill, and so, in an unprecedented military operation, neither the adversary nor the Malvinas population suffered a single casualty.'[5]

It was, as it happened, Britain and not Argentina that made the next significant move escalating the conflict. Both the nature and the timing of the move were in the highest degree unfortunate; both seeming to the uncommitted and the unsympathetic as dramatic evidence that Britain and not Argentina was the true aggressor.

At 3.00 p.m. local time on 3 May a British nuclear-powered submarine, HMS *Conqueror*, sighted the Argentine cruiser, the 13,645 ton *General Belgrano*, close to Isla de los Estados, some 240 miles from the Falklands and hence outside the 200 mile exclusion zone. Believing, having shadowed it for some hours, that it was a potential threat to British naval operations, and acting directly under orders from Northwood under the general warning that ships so engaged were liable to be sunk, it fired two Tigerfish wire-guided torpedoes at the cruiser, which was immediately seen to be seriously damaged. It deliberately did not attack the cruiser's two escorting destroyers, but as the sea around the sinking cruiser blossomed with orange liferafts, the escorts fled from the scene, and by the time they returned to offer help it was already certain that a substantial number of the *Belgrano*'s crew would be lost. As the military authorities in Buenos Aires were unwilling, and possibly unable, to state how many men had been on board the cruiser, initial estimates of the losses ranged up to 600 or more. In fact, owing to the fact that the cruiser sank within forty minutes of the explosion, having almost immediately developed a severe list, the final figure of 368 was still very high. It was, in fact, the most serious event of the entire campaign, and, not surprisingly, it galvanised the Argentine authorities into furious military and diplomatic action.[6]

Hence, though the initial reaction in Britain was to see the sinking of the *General Belgrano* as a further step in making the blockade effective, its effect was in fact to ensure that the blockade, even if effective (which it was not), would not and could not by itself bring Britain the goals for which it had been established.

The sinking was denounced by the Argentine Government as 'a treacherous act of aggression'. Ignoring the so-called Defensive Zone around the task force vessels, and drawing attention to the fact that the incident had occurred, by its reckoning, thirty-six miles outside the 200 mile exclusion zone, the Argentines claimed that up to that point their forces had acted only in self-defence. It was now Britain that, by this act of aggression, was in breach of Security Council Resolution 502.[7] And this view was shared elsewhere in the world. The Fianna Faíl Government of Mr Charles Haughey, never noted for its sympathy towards British policy and sustained only by the slenderest of majorities, took Ireland into the international arena by seeking an immediate meeting of the Security Council to try to halt the fighting. Its resolution, calling for an immediate cessation of hostilities and the negotiation of a diplomatic settlement under United Nations auspices, would have consolidated the Argentine occupation of the Falklands.[8] What sort of reception it might have received in the Security Council might be gauged from President Brezhnev of the Soviet Union, who likened the action to 'colonial brigandage' in a toast to the Nicaraguan leader, Sr Daniel Ortega.[9]

A strong suspicion that a further meeting of the Security Council might be made to look ridiculous, if its resolutions were again disregarded, delayed action on the Irish request. In Brussels, however, its further request that EEC sanctions on Argentina should be lifted met with sympathy from delegates shocked at the news of the sinking and the high casualties, and already impatient with Britain's dogged attitude towards its budget contributions and the common agricultural policy. While French spokesmen privately voiced their concern, publicly they stated that their Government's position had in no way changed, and that it was intolerable that Argentina had tried to take the law into its own hands. But Dutch and West German attitudes were less firm, and Britain's new ally, the United States, was cautious. 'One could readily reach the conclusion that the recent tragic loss of lives associated with the loss of their cruiser has contributed to their continuing intransigence', Mr Haig said of Argentina to the Senate Appropriations Committee.[10]

But the ability of Argentina to capitalise on this shift in world opinion proved to be limited. To do so, it would have had to hold back a military response, and internal pressures probably made that impossible. At any rate, news of the rising total of survivors from the *General Belgrano* was soon overtaken in the headlines by the news of a major naval disaster for Britain. So sudden and unexpected was it, that even in Buenos Aires the news was treated with the greatest caution, and not confirmed by military sources until well after the confirmation by the Defence Ministry in London.

Late in the afternoon of Tuesday 4 May, the pilot of an Argentine Super-Etendard aircraft, one of three of the newly delivered, French built aircraft which had been sent to mount an air attack on the British task force, detected a small radar blip in the expected position, some sixty miles south of the Falklands. He and another pilot each fired their Exocet air-to-surface missiles from a distance of some twenty-three miles, and then turned away. They were therefore unaware of the consequences. The surface-skimming missile (the name means 'flying fish' in French) dropped to its assigned height of some 15 feet (4.5 m) above the waves and, guided by its inbuilt homing guidance system, headed for the destroyer HMS *Sheffield*, undetected by the ship's own radar system. The crew of the ship, which was said subsequently not to have been at action stations, had no more than a few seconds warning of the approaching missile, which entered the ship on the starboard side still some 15 feet above the waterline and exploded within the main bulk of the ship close to the control room.[11]

The *Sheffield* was one of the newest ships in the force. The first of the 3,660 ton Type-42 destroyers, when it was launched in 1971 it had aroused considerable controversy. For on the one hand it represented a revolution in warship design, abandoning the old idea of heavy armour plated static protection in favour of a small light hull, with light-weight aluminium superstructure to house the Sea Dart missile system together with its associated radars and electronic countermeasures. On the other, it had been built down to a price, and because of this its hull had been 40 feet shorter than originally planned. Hence it had not been possible to fit *Sheffield* with the later anti-missile-missile systems or extend the range of its armament.[12]

The extent of the disaster that now befell the *Sheffield*, however, took almost everyone by surprise. Within seconds the ship filled with thick suffocating smoke as fire spread from end to end of the vessel. Despite energetic damage control measures it proved impossible to contain it. After four hours the order had to be given to abandon ship; many of the crew leaping to safety on to the deck of a frigate, HMS *Arrow*, which at great risk to itself had come alongside to give assistance.[13] In the circumstances it was indeed fortunate that as few as twenty lives were lost. Amid the rough seas the ship burnt on for no less than seven days until, after attempts to take her in tow, it was decided to accept that she was beyond salvaging.[14]

On board the British task force the result was an increased respect for the Argentines in general, and its air force in particular. As a petty officer on board HMS *Invincible* was reported to have said: 'Everyone thought we were taking on a bunch of bean eaters but now they realize they are up against a well-equipped outfit.'[15]

In London the initial effect was one of alarm. Ironically, exchanges earlier in the day in the House of Commons had placed the Government on the defensive over the sinking of the *General Belgrano*. Mr Healey had then demanded to know just how far the Argentine cruiser was from the task force, and whether the submarine had sought to cripple rather than sink it. In reply, Mr Nott had been unconvincing, saying only that it was only 'hours steaming time away,' which suggested distance rather than proximity, and then taking refuge in operational silence.[16] It had been Mrs Thatcher who had earlier reminded Mr Foot of that warning given to the Argentine Government on 23 April, that 'any approach . . . which could amount to a threat to interfere with the mission of British forces in the South Atlantic' would 'encounter the appropriate response.' It was also she who, when pressed by Mr Foot as to why 'the maximum force or a very considerable amount of force' had been used against the cruiser, stated bluntly:

May I make it perfectly clear that the worry I live with hourly is that attacking Argentine forces either naval or air, may get through to ours and sink some of our ships. I am sure that will also be in the right hon. Gentleman's mind.

There was clear aggressive intent by the Argentine fleet and government. It could be seen first in their claims. They previously claimed that they had sunk HMS 'Exeter,' that they had damaged HMS 'Hermes' leaving it inoperative and badly damaged, and that they had brought down 11 Harriers. That was clear evidence of Argentine aggressive intent. The right hon. Gentleman may also remember the persistent attacks throughout the whole of Saturday [1 May] on the task force, which were only repelled by the supreme skill and courage of our people.[17]

Now that the contingency the Prime Minister had feared had actually arisen, demands by the Opposition to clarify the extent of political control of military decisions were speedily allowed to lapse, though not before the Defence Secretary's inability to confirm or deny further reports of fighting in the South Atlantic demonstrated that they had had every reason for concern. New interest in the possibilities of diplomacy were expressed by Mr Pym. 'The military losses which have now occurred on both sides in this unhappy conflict emphasise all the more the urgent need to find a diplomatic solution', he asserted, at the beginning of a statement in which he made it clear that diplomacy, even if it had received less attention in the preceding days than was its due, was still proceeding.[18] With the collapse of the Haig Mission, the Peruvian peace plan had moved to centre stage, and it is clear, even if Mr Pym did not say so, that Britain was under even stronger pressure to be seen to negotiate, especially in the United States where the sinking of the *Sheffield* cast serious doubts on whether the task force was really capable of securing a forceful solution, even if that were diplomatically desirable.[19]

So it was to the Peruvian peace plan that the British Government, deeply conscious of the sudden erosion of its diplomatic position, and very much on the defensive, now turned its attention.

There were three main points to the plan, which had been put forward by President Fernando Belaúnde Terry of Peru the previous Saturday and which was based on earlier suggestions of a similar nature, as well as the Haig proposals themselves. But in essence it had three main points. An immediate seventy-two hour truce should be called. This would be followed by the withdrawal of both Argentine and British forces from the area. Negotiations, probably under United Nations auspices, would then take place on the ultimate future of the islands. As the Peruvian Ambassador to Washington pointed out, the proposals had originally not attracted much interest from Mr Pym.[20] What he omitted to say was that they had not then either attracted much attention from the Argentines. It was now hoped that with American support for the proposals, and implicitly the guarantee that they would be honoured by Britain, they might be acceptable in Buenos Aires. But in fact after informal discussions with Argentine representatives in Lima, the Peruvian Government found on Thursday 8 May, that they were still unacceptable there, and that the Junta was not prepared to contemplate withdrawal.[21]

A major weakness of the Peruvian plan, which would almost certainly have prejudiced its acceptance, was the absence of a mediating figure to command the respect and attention of both sides, and to ensure the completion of the process once begun. The breakdown of the initiative now focused attention on the only remaining person who could fulfil this role: the Secretary General of the United Nations.

The Secretary General's good offices

As Mr Pym was blaming 'Argentine intransigence' for frustrating 'a constructive initiative' that could, he said, have led to a ceasefire from 5.00 p.m. BST on Friday 7 May, observers were already digesting the implications of a further statement by Mrs Thatcher in the House of Commons. 'We welcome the ideas that the Secretary General has put forward and can accept them as a framework on which more specific proposals could be built,' she said. 'We are sending a message to the Secretary General today to that effect.'[22] She added a warning that it was possible that the Argentines were seeking a ceasefire without withdrawal, and made it clear that anything less than the full implementation of Resolution 502 would be unacceptable to the British Government.

Stating that Argentina's aim was to seek a peaceful solution, Dr Costa Méndez remained in Buenos Aires himself, but dispatched the Under Secretary of the Argentine Foreign Ministry, the career civil servant Dr Enrique Ros, to New

York to discuss the position with the Secretary General.[23] It will be recalled that it was Dr Ros who had had the task of conducting the fateful talks with Mr Richard Luce, and who had failed to warn him of the possible consequences of them. From the Argentine point of view, the merit of the Secretary General's ideas was precisely their imprecise and unformed nature. They comprised six points: an immediate end to hostilities, withdrawal of Argentine troops from the islands, withdrawal of the British fleet, opening of negotiations on the future of the islands, the ending of economic sanctions against Argentina, and the establishment of a joint administration of the islands under United Nations auspices.[24] But at this initial stage they lacked specific points of detail, and, above all, they lacked any agreed timetable. Apart from the authority lent to them by the Secretary General, therefore, they were much less likely to be acceptable to the British Government than the Haig proposals or the Peruvian peace plan, incomplete in many respects as those were. Like the good diplomat that he was, however, the Secretary General had waited until the moment at which his good offices could command the full and undivided diplomatic attention of the combatants. He therefore found that he obtained an encouraging response from his first talks both with Dr Ros and with Sir Anthony Parsons on behalf of the British Government (7 May).

Britain, as Mr Pym was quick to point out in the House, had stated in response to the Peruvian proposals that it was 'willing to accept and implement immediately an interim agreement which would prepare the way for a definitive settlement'. For this reason he was sceptical of Argentine claims now to be accepting the Secretary General's ideas. Despite this Britain had now sent him 'a positive and substantive reply'

I made it clear at the same time that in our view Resolution 502 must be implemented without delay; that an unconditional ceasefire could not under any circumstances be regarded by us as a step towards this; and that implementation of a ceasefire must be unambiguously linked to the commencement of Argentine withdrawal, which must be completed within a fixed number of days.

Pressed by Mr Healey to state that he would not 'seek to

broaden the conflict', and in particular to reject the idea put forward by a small group of Conservative backbenchers that Britain should bomb Argentine airbases on the mainland, the Foreign Secretary gave a guarded answer, which tended to heighten rather than allay concern on the matter. In retrospect, however, it is plain that the mainland bombing project had never been seriously considered in Government circles, and that the statement was meant to imply rejection:

I assure the right hon. Gentleman that we have no desire to escalate military action, let alone to broaden the field of military activity. Clearly, our concern is to confine it. At this point one cannot rule out any option. That must not be taken by the House to mean anything specific.[25]

What was done instead, in the light of the experience of the *Sheffield*, was spectacular enough and virtually without precedent in a state of undeclared war. This was the warning, issued at 6.00 p.m. the same evening by the official spokesman at the Ministry of Defence, Mr Ian McDonald, that British forces would henceforth treat as hostile all Argentine ships and aircraft detected more than twelve miles off the Argentine coast.[26] The decision to make such an announcement at such a time, however valuable it might be in gaining precious seconds of warning for the task force ships, was crassly insensitive to world opinion and its arrogance drove the Junta to a furious response, calling it — accurately — 'a belligerent action, which can only escalate the conflict and the dangers of renewed hostilities'. What made it all the more extraordinary was the fact that it denied Argentine ships and vessels the right to use 188 miles of the 200 mile limit that their Government, as those of almost all the major Latin American countries, had claimed for over a decade. It was therefore stretching Britain's case to be acting within international law to the limit, if not beyond, and it generated more than a little suspicion that the British Government did not take the Secretary General's good offices sufficiently seriously.[27]

This feeling was reinforced when, on Sunday 9 May, it was British forces that broke five days' lull in hostilities by shelling military installations at Port Stanley, and attacking an Argentine fishing vessel that had been shadowing the fleet. The vessel, the *Narwal*, was strafed and captured. Its crew were found to include an Argentine naval officer, and captured records showed that the suspicions of spying that had prompted the attack were correct. But in the meantime, as part of an exotic growth of propaganda and rumour in Buenos Aires, the British were accused of having tried to machinegun the survivors, a story which to their discredit, some of them repeated later after their safe repatriation via Montevideo to Argentina.[28]

Despite the unpropitious beginning, the talks in New York went ahead, the Secretary General appearing from time to time to utter statements of cautious optimism to waiting newsmen and television cameras. In a television interview screened on 9 May, Dr Costa Méndez stated that it was not necessary for Britain to recognise Argentine sovereignty over the islands at the outset of negotiations, and this was widely reported as a concession. But he also made it clear that any negotiation must eventually lead to recognition by Britain of Argentine sovereignty; as British officials warned, hardly a concession.[29] By Tuesday 11 May, the British Government had let it be known that it was resigned to the talks lasting at least another week.[30] Meanwhile hostilities were restricted by bad weather conditions, though the task force continued to build up its strength in the vicinity of the islands. On the British side, some twenty more Harriers had successfully made the direct flight from Ascension Island over the weekend, refuelling in flight.[31] On the Argentine side, flights resumed on 12 May, when two Skyhawks were shot down by Sea Wolf missiles.[32] But the situation remained under control while the talks continued.

The first break in the apparently smooth flow of the talks came on 13 May, when it was disclosed in Washington that the sovereignty issue remained unresolved. 'Britain and Argentina have moved closer on peripherals, but not on the issue of sovereignty', a high Washington official stated, and it was disclosed that President Reagan had again sent General Vernon Walters to Buenos Aires with proposals for resolving that part of the dispute. Since he had already publicly described the crisis as 'a silly war and a conflict of egos', and had said of Mrs Thatcher that 'the machismo of women is even more sensitive than the machismo of men', the good reception given in Buenos Aires to his ideas was not warmly welcomed by British diplomatic staff in Washington.[33] By the weekend Sr Pérez de Cuellar was denying that he contemplated 'endless negotiations' and his staff were emphasising that much work still had to be done on filling in the points of detail,[34] and on the Friday evening, 14 May, speaking to the annual conference of Scottish Conservatives in Perth, Mrs Thatcher warned that a 'negotiated settlement' of the dispute, for all the work that had been done, might 'prove unattainable.'[35] Meanwhile Press reports stated that the task force was now ready to launch an action to repossess the islands, and that there was growing confidence both there and at home that such an action could be carried out effectively and without undue casualties, something that had previously been held in some doubt, given the difficulty of achieving satisfactory air cover for a long enough period.

What the Secretary General had done, it appeared, was to deal with all the easy questions first and to leave the really difficult ones to be resolved between the parties in later negotiations. Three main problems still remained to be resolved. Britain wanted assurances that the question of sovereignty would not be conceded at the start of negotiations, and the wishes of the islanders would be taken into account in any final agreement on the future of the islands. Argentina wanted a time limit on negotiations, so that Britain could not prolong the talks indefinitely, and for this reason it was unwilling to accept any arrangement for extending the talks beyond the original proposed period of six months or a year.[36] But the British Government, for its part, feared with reason that if the talks broke down, in six months time after the task force had been recalled, there would be the greatest difficulty in resisting any new seizure of the islands.

In London the Government was already having difficulties with its own supporters, some of whom were beginning, as they thought, to scent a 'sell-out'. Suspicions that the Foreign Office were prepared to go too far in appeasing the Argentines gained strength in the course of Thursday 13 May, when there were noticeable discrepancies between the answers given to questioners by Mr Pym in the fifth major debate on the crisis and those offered earlier by Mrs Thatcher.[37] Mrs Thatcher in response to questioning had been quite definite that the task force would not be withdrawn until the Argentine forces had left. Mr Pym appeared to be prepared to accept a joint phased withdrawal. Mr Pym on the other hand stated that the question of sovereignty must not be prejudged while the Prime Minister, stating that it was 'negotiable', seemed only to rule out an immediate concession of sovereignty. This apparent hint of concession on this fundamental issue was then taken up by the former Prime Minister, Mr Edward Heath, who, while stressing the identity he saw between his views and those of Mr Pym, specifically recommended him to give the Argentine Government 'some way out', and recalled how President John Kennedy of the United States had done so to the Soviet Union at the time of the Cuban Missile Crisis of 1962. In both this and his argument that the islanders should not any longer be allowed a 'veto' on a settlement, his views came close to those of Mr Healey and Dr Owen, and the former argued in the debate that though the task force must not be withdrawn, Britain must equally be prepared to make concessions and not be swayed by the 'strident voices from the militarist tendency'.[38]

Again in retrospect, it seems surprising that more emphasis at the time was not placed on the words of the Foreign Secretary's statement, which suggested a very different interpretation. Only the first signs of willingness to negotiate had been shown by Argentina; much more was still needed. Economic sanctions were crucial. 'Europe remains on our side', he said. But while talks went on Britain would continue to tighten the military screw:

We all grieve over British losses. We take no satisfaction at the losses inflicted on Argentina. We regret them, too, but as the net closes round the islands military incidents may occur with increasing frequency. That may be inevitable in the circumstances. But we must never forget who is the aggressor, who invaded whom, who embarked on an unlawful and dangerous course, who first took up arms and thus put lives at risk, who fired the first shot. Argentina knows how to avoid further military conflict. It can begin its withdrawal now.[39]

that for the fourth weekend in a row there would be some
spectacular military development — it was in danger of
becoming a settled pattern of the British campaign. In the
circumstances it was remarkable that once again tactical
surprise was achieved. The target for what was described
as 'the most intense British naval bombardment since the
Second World War' was the Argentine airbase on Pebble
Island, a small island off the north of West Falkland close
to the entrance to Falkland Sound. But the bombardment
was only cover and support for a daring Commando raid
which blew up no fewer than eleven aircraft and destroyed
strategic radar installations and an ammunition dump which
could have impeded a landing anywhere in the immediate
area.[40] But the destruction of these facilities was essential
for a successful landing on the site that had already been
reconnoitred and selected. Indeed, as persistent press reports
had not failed to disclose, reconnaissance teams had been
landing by boat and air at various points in the islands from
1–2 May onward, sending back vital intelligence on enemy
strengths and dispositions.[41] And as winter advanced and
the weather became both worse and more unpredictable, the
advice reaching London was that a landing looked increasingly
practicable, while a long drawn-out blockade, such as that
initially favoured by Labour spokesmen in the House, presented hazards to naval vessels that were even more serious
than had at first been feared.

The Pebble Island raid, therefore, like the first bombardment of Port Stanley, followed military logic and took its
place in the unfolding military timetable. But ironically
it was not so much the raid as the legacy of the *General
Belgrano* which was to ensure that in under a week Britain
would have only the military option left of those it had
originally developed.

It was the economic consensus that gave way first. Sanctions
throughout the period of their use had always been more
symbolic than real. The problem was that most of them took
so long to work. Even military supplies had been flown out
of Stansted Airport bound for Argentina only two days
before the invasion of the islands,[42] and most commercial
cargoes were still in transit long after that. The financial

interests of the City of London could, single handed, have demolished Argentine foreign credit without reference to others. But this, it was agreed alike in Britain, Europe and the United States, might bring down the whole elaborate structure of international lending with unpredictable results. It was European solidarity, not European pressure, that had so far had most effect, and the sanctions now had to be renewed from midnight on 17 April if they were going to have time to work.

But despite Mr Pym's confident assertion to the House of Commons Europe's support could no longer be taken for granted. After the attack on the *General Belgrano* Ireland, Denmark and West Germany had all expressed concern about the use of force, and, as we have seen, Ireland took the further step of requesting Community foreign ministers to end the sanctions there and then. Their argument was that as a neutral country, Ireland had supported sanctions as an alternative to force, not as an aid to force. The acceptance by Britain of the good offices of the Secretary General had brought some relief, but then the mounting toll of casualties, and the effect of Argentine family ties with German and Italian connections, both began to be felt.

On 16 May the Cabinet met at Chequers for the second time in twenty-four hours to discuss reports from the British Ambassadors to the United Nations and to Washington on the progress of the Secretary General's efforts. Mr Pym flew from that meeting directly to Luxembourg for the meeting of EEC foreign ministers, where he was able to give assurances that the negotiations were still in progress. Despite this it was clear that unity was not attainable, and the meeting adjourned that night without taking a decision on whether to renew sanctions or not.[43] On the following day, Monday 17 May, the deadlock could not be resolved, and in the end, under the provisions of the so-called 'Luxembourg Compromise', Italy declared that it regarded the question of the unanimous renewal of sanctions to be a matter of important national interest, and so vetoed the renewal of sanctions as unanimous Community policy.[44] In a later evening meeting, however, the ministers agreed to renew sanctions for one week only on a voluntary basis, a face-saving gesture which left the British representative little comfort. Certainly what there was was swept away the following day, when the ministers joined ranks against Britain to abandon the 'Luxembourg Compromise' on the farm price increases proposed by the Commission, only to try to renew it again after they had finished.[45]

On the same day, Monday 17 May, Sir Anthony Parsons had returned to New York with fresh instructions to continue the negotiations. His return coincided with the latest formal reply of the Junta to the Secretary General. Though this altogether avoided mention of the issue of sovereignty, and so gave rise to some optimism in New York, that optimism was not shared in London, for the insistence on ultimate control of the islands remained. Worse still, it was clear that the Argentine Government would not allow any part in the interim administration of the islands to the islanders, which was of course wholly in keeping with its attitude towards the Argentinians themselves, but was quite unacceptable to the British Government.[46] To obtain clarification of the outstanding issues, on which the British Government regarded the Junta as being deliberately vague, Sir Anthony now presented Britain's final negotiating position to the Secretary General.

Meanwhile the speeches of the members of the Junta suggested that they were united by only one thing: a growing awareness that further military conflict was likely. On Navy Day Admiral Anaya said, in the course of a long soliloquy to the serried ranks of naval officers: 'We are the protagonists of a historical event we did not seek or instigate. However it has allowed us — the Argentine people and mankind as a whole — to understand the real essence of the world we live in, where arrogance and haughtiness are no longer accepted.'[47] The Commander of the Air Force, Brigadier Lami Dozo was more forthright: 'Our position has not changed. Perhaps we are using different words but our attitude is the same. . . .'[48]

First indications of the Argentine response to the British proposals were received in London on the morning of 19 May, and by the same evening the full response had been received in writing. It confirmed that the British proposals had been wholly rejected. As Mrs Thatcher told a crowded House of Commons on the afternoon of 20 May: 'Indeed, in many respects the Argentine reply went back to their position when they rejected Mr Haig's second set of proposals on 29 April.'[49]

In this statement she presented the British Government's definitive position on the successive negotiations so far and why in its view the talks had now broken down. Four sets of proposals had been considered during the Haig Mission; the last had been rejected by Argentina. A fifth had then been presented by the President of Peru; that had been rejected by Argentina. All those sets of proposals had now been withdrawn. Then, following discussions with the Secretary General of the United Nations, the Government had, the previous Monday, presented a draft interim agreement to him, making it clear that 'the text represented the furthest that Britain could go in the negotiations'. It had requested a reply within forty-eight hours. That reply 'amounted to a rejection'.

The British proposals, Mrs Thatcher made clear, preserved the fundamental principles of the Government's position: 'Aggression must not be allowed to succeed; International law must be upheld; Sovereignty cannot be changed by invasion.'

The liberty of the Falkland islanders must be restored. For years they have been free to express their own wishes about how they want to be governed. They have had institutions of their own choosing. They have enjoyed self-determination. Why should they lose that freedom and exchange it for dictatorship?

The proposals were contained in two documents. One, a letter to the Secretary General, made it clear that the draft interim agreement did not apply to South Georgia and the South Sandwich Islands. The other, the draft interim agreement, concerned the Falklands only. On the signature of the agreement, the forces of both sides were to withdraw to a distance of at least 150 nautical miles from the islands within fourteen days. A United Nations administrator, appointed by the Secretary General from among persons acceptable to both Britain and Argentina, would verify the withdrawal. He would be empowered to prevent their return with the aid of a small force drawn from three or four other countries, and would administer the islands in consultation with the Islands Executive and Legislative Councils, to each of which would be added one member representative of the twenty or so Argentines normally resident on the islands. Then negotiations would be held on the long term future of the islands. 'Those negotiations shall be initiated without prejudice to the rights, claims and positions of the parties and without prejudgement of the outcome.'

This interim agreement therefore represented substantial concessions on Britain's part without infringing the fundamental principles outlined above. The Argentine reply, on the other hand, raised all the points 'which had been obstacles in earlier negotiations'.

Their proposals were that South Georgia and the South Sandwich Islands should be included in any agreement; that all forces should withdraw and return to 'their normal bases and areas of operation'; the withdrawal, moreover, including withdrawal of troops from South Georgia, which would plainly leave Britain at an enormous disadvantage. Administration of the islands would be exclusively in the hands of a UN Administrator. He would be advised by a council containing equal numbers of British and Argentine residents of the islanders, despite the fact that there were 1,780 of the former to only 20 of the latter, and that Argentines would in the interim period have equal access to the islands with regard to 'residence, work and property'. For the long term, the settlement must conform not only with the Charter of the United Nations, 'but with various resolutions of the General Assembly, from some of which the United Kingdom dissented on the grounds that they favoured Argentine sovereignty'. It would be the General Assembly that would determine the ultimate fate of the islands if in the negotiations Britain and Argentina failed to agree.

It was manifestly impossible for Britain to accept such demands. Argentina began this crisis. Argentina has rejected proposal after proposal. One is bound to ask whether the junta have ever intended to seek a peaceful settlement or whether they have sought merely to confuse and prolong the negotiations while remaining in illegal possession of the islands.

And of the British Government's own proposals she said flatly: 'The proposals have been rejected. They are no longer on the table.'

Mrs Thatcher dealt more kindly with the Secretary General's own attempts to identify those areas on which agreement already existed, saying only that one of them, the holding of negotiations without prejudgement, was 'belied by a succession of statements from Buenos Aires'. She was much sharper with Mr Foot when he sought, as he had earlier, to persuade her to 'give every proper response to the Secretary General', saying that 'in the months ahead' Britain would need all the support it could get in the United Nations. Mr Foot got a quick rebuff, and, led by Mr Benn, the Member for Bristol South-East, a small group of Labour MPs for the first time in the crisis broke the unity of the House by forcing a division, in which, however, they were defeated by 296 votes to thirty-three.[50]

The Argentine Foreign Office was subsequently to claim that its reply had been intended, not as a rejection, but as a request for clarification.[51] This argument was disingenuous. There could be no mistake, in the circumstances, about the fact that Britain was presenting in effect an ultimatum, nor indeed had there been any doubt in Buenos Aires in the previous week that this was the case. Possible options for a British attack on the islands were already being discussed there, and intelligence sources who could do no more than read the British press were fully aware that for several days the task force had been at operational strength and readiness.[52]

Up to the previous weekend it seems that in the inner Cabinet there was still hope that the Secretary General's efforts might lead to a breakthrough, and that, even if the chance was slight, every attempt should be made to secure an agreement. The Luxembourg decision, certainly, left Britain so weakened diplomatically, that the well-meaning efforts of Ireland and Italy to avert conflict might seem to have succeeded in producing exactly the result they were trying to avoid. But by then it had already been decided to put the Argentine Government to the test, diplomatically speaking, and to publish the breakdown of negotiations as a prelude to a military landing. The intent to carry out such a landing had, after all, been present from the day the ships sailed, otherwise they would have not included among their number such a proportion of assault and similar vessels. If it was not stated as the goal of the operation at that stage, this was undoubtedly partly for diplomatic reasons, but it was also because until the local conditions were assessed, it could not be said authoritatively how high the chances were of ultimate success. Lastly, the decision on 3 May to requisition the QE2, with her unique size and speed, meant that at any time after the expiry of the ultimatum, the task force commander would be able to call in addition on substantial reserves in the shape of the 5th Infantry Brigade, and raised the odds on the landing's success to what was confidently hoped would be an acceptable level. The withdrawal of all earlier proposals, far from being just a piece of obscurantism as some Opposition spokesmen seemed to think, then became an essential safeguard for Britain's future diplomatic position in the event of military success. For having refused previously to abide by the first two parts of Resolution 502 it was not the intention of the British Government that the Argentines would then be able to invoke the third. In other words, the ending of the negotiations on the future of the islands was final.

Repossessing the islands

As dawn rose on East Falkland on the morning of Friday 21 May 1982, it disclosed an astonishing sight. Just after midnight, as the news came of the breakdown of negotiations in New York, the signal had been given for the planned landing to take place and forty ships had set their course along the northern coast of the island and into Falkland Sound. There, in San Carlos Water, they had begun to discharge their troops and cargoes, while to the East of Port Stanley, HMS *Hermes* and *Invincible* launched heavy Harrier raids on Stanley and Goose Green. These, together with a commando raid on Fox Bay in West Falkland, were designed to confuse and bemuse the Argentine garrisons, and if possible to convince them that the expected landing was taking place in the south.

The diversions were wholly successful, though Mr Nott's claim at the time that the landings were unopposed was not entirely correct. No Argentine troops were on hand to try to stop the first troops coming ashore, and the small garrison of Port San Carlos was swiftly overrun. By dawn a thousand men were already forming a beachhead, and tanks, armoured cars and missile batteries had been landed. Shortly afterwards, with a defensive screen of destroyers and frigates already drawn up in the inlet, protecting the troop ship *Canberra* and the assault ships, *Fearless* and *Intrepid*, the rest of the civilian support vessels entered the inlet to unload. By 10.00 a.m. three hours after first light, the landing was still proceeding, though by now well advanced and secured against any likely ground attack.

The counter-attack, however, came, as expected, from the air. First came the Pucara ground-attack planes, still numerous despite the raid on Pebble Island. Then came the Skyhawks and Mirages from the Argentine mainland. The landing site had been deliberately chosen so that the hills round about would leave them as little room as possible, with the result that their main attack was aimed not at the troops on the ground, but at the ships in the bay. Five of them were hit. The frigate HMS *Ardent* was hit by bombs and rockets and caught fire, sinking later with the loss of twenty-two lives. Two more were killed in the attacks on the other ships. But ironically the worst losses of the day, which saw the *Canberra* herself straddled by two 1,000 lb bombs, had already occurred before dawn, when a Sea King helicopter transferring troops into the landing craft had ditched with the loss of thirty-one crew and passengers. In reply the Argentines, continuing to fly sorties until darkness fell, lost nine Mirages, five Skyhawks and two Pucaras, as well as four helicopters.[53]

The Argentines did not admit these heavy losses, but they did not return in force on the Saturday, thus allowing a crucial extra day for the landing forces to consolidate their beachhead and to set up their Rapier anti-aircraft missile batteries on the surrounding hills.[54] But when they did return on the afternoon of Sunday 23 May, it was to launch a massive attack with more than forty aircraft on the British fleet. Two bombs hit HMS *Antelope* but failed to explode, and she was able to steam off to a new anchorage where attempts could be made to defuse one which had lodged in the engineroom. It was at 6.00 p.m., well after dark, that the bomb exploded, killing the man who was working on it. Though the ship blazed furiously all night until a further explosion broke her back and sunk her the next morning, all the rest of the crew were safely rescued from her blazing decks. HMS *Argonaut* was luckier. Bombs had crippled her motive power so that she was unable to move, but her armament remained fully effective, and she survived the day; on 27 May, while repair work was in progress, she too went on fire, but this time, despite further air attacks, helicopter-borne assistance succeeded in putting the fire out. As ITN commentator Michael Nicholson later said: 'It continued to astonish us how fast fire spread on a modern warship.'[55] The accompanying hazards were no less serious. Lieutenant Richard Govan of the *Antelope* reported 'thick, choking black smoke, and molten aluminium falling on the flight deck'.[56]

By 25 May, the Argentine National Day, reinforcements for the ships had arrived in the form of the Type-82 guided-missile destroyer HMS *Bristol* and supporting vessels.[57] With something of a respite on 24 May to assist, there were now nearly 5,000 men ashore, and the perimeter of the beach-head was being extended in all directions. It had yet, however, to meet any ground-based counter-attack. So although the day, from the British point of view, was to prove the most serious so far, it did mark a major turning point in the campaign. From then on the forces could go on the offensive, provided that the long line of logistic supply could be maintained. But it was precisely this need that the sinking of the *Atlantic Conveyor* momentarily put in doubt.

The *Atlantic Conveyor* appears to have been mistaken by the Argentine pilot of a Super-Etendard for an aircraft carrier for she was not in the Falkland Sound or its vicinity at the time. Given the size of her 'blip' on the radar screen, it would have been a natural mistake. Like the *Sheffield*, she was hit by an Exocet missile, one of two fired by aircraft

well out of visual range.[58] Fortuantely she had already discharged her cargo of Sea Harriers, but important stores
remained on board, including heavy Chinook helicopters
and probably a portable airstrip. Some of them were later
salvaged from the burning vessel before she sank. This action
almost exhausted the stock of some five air-to-surface Exocets
that had been delivered to Argentina before her invasion and
the imposition of the French arms sales ban. In the course
of the next three weeks Argentina was believed to have
obtained replacement missiles via Peru, but they arrived in
the event too late to change the outcome of the campaign.[59]

The Type-42 destroyer HMS *Coventry* was hit by several
bombs from Argentine Skyhawks shortly before darkness
fell on a day on which her Sea Dart missile systems had
enabled her, from an exposed warning position at the opening into the Sound, to help bring down up to five aircraft.
She capsised shortly after the attack with the loss of a
further twenty lives; the losses of the day bringing the British
total to 100.[60]

Further raids on 27 May failed to secure any further
successes on the fleet, but damaged the field hospital at Ajax
Bay where both British and Argentine casualties were being
treated, and continued to be treated, under the most difficult conditions imaginable. But already the successes of the
preceding days had given the Argentines every reason for
optimism. With news of the British naval losses confirmed
from London attention was distracted from the air losses,
which, like the number of British troops successfully disembarked on the island, were systematically underestimated
in a stream of victorious communiqués. Best of all, from the
Argentine point of view, the opening of the military campaign
on land had brought them a striking diplomatic triumph.

Within hours of the landings on 21 May Dr Costa Méndez
had called for a meeting of the Security Council which
Britain, anxious to avert any resolution that might hamper
plans for a landing, had hitherto successfully blocked. With
Ireland's request for a meeting already on the table, it was
now swiftly convened, and Dr Costa Méndez set off from
Buenos Aires to attend it. In the meantime a long queue of
Latin American states lined up to denounce British aggression

and state their support for the Argentine claims to the
islands. Only one of them, Panama, was a member of the
Council and so able to vote, but from the beginning it was
apparent that for its part Britain lacked unequivocal support, particularly from the United States. Its Ambassador,
the redoubtable Mrs Jeane Kirkpatrick, did indeed speak
of her country's 'unique ties' with Britain, but she also
called Argentina 'an old friend with which we share the
enormous human and national potential of the New World
experience'.[61]

It was to these prejudices that the Argentine Foreign
Minister addressed himself in his speech on 25 May, speaking
of Argentina's 'rights', reminding his eager audience of
Britain's colonial past, and blaming it for its intransigence
towards a weaker opponent: 'My country is at this moment
resisting an invasion. It is doing so with all the means at its
disposal and by the determination and the courage and
patriotism of its people.'[62]

Significantly, whatever his inner feelings, he was con-
spicuously careful to utter only a mild rebuke to the United
States. In so doing he played on the developing split in the
State Department between the Ambassador, deeply concerned for the future of United States security if Latin
America were alienated, and Mr Haig, who, expecting a
British victory, had already called on Mrs Thatcher to be
'magnanimous'.[63] He did not specifically ask for a ceasefire.
But that had already been suggested by among others,
Ireland, Panama and Brazil, in each case in a way that was
likely to prove unacceptable to Britain, which gave notice
that if pressed it would veto a resolution with which it did
not agree. The result was a resolution, sponsored by Guayana,
Ireland, Jordan, Togo, Uganda and Zaïre, which simply
renewed the Secretary General's mandate to use his good
offices and called upon him to report within seven days on
the progress of his negotiations to bring about a ceasefire.
The resolution was adopted without dissent.[64]

But before this happened Argentina had also demanded
and obtained a meeting of the Foreign Ministers of the
Organization of American States.[65] Here, behind closed
doors, a forty-five minute tirade from Dr Costa Méndez

against the United States for 'supporting the criminal colonialist, warlike adventure' of Britain, was greeted with a standing ovation. There was, it was true, even some applause for Mr Haig, who repeated that Argentina had been the first to use force and that hence there was no case for supporting it under the Rio Treaty, and added, more tellingly, that it was Argentina, not Britain, that had rejected his initiative of 27 April and the subsequent Peruvian peace plan.[66] But the meeting ended with an overwhelming vote, of seventeen to none with four abstentions, for a resolution condemning Britain's attack on the islands, urging the United States to halt aid to Britain and calling on members to offer any aid to Argentina they thought appropriate — a resolution, indeed, that only thanks to heavy United States lobbying stopped short of calling for collective mandatory sanctions against Britain. The abstainers were the United States, Chile, Colombia and Trinidad and Tobago.

It was at this point that the row between Mr Haig and Mrs Kirkpatrick became public. In a 'heated 45-minute telephone conversation' she was said to have called him and his aides 'amateurs . . . totally insensitive to Latin cultures', and denounced what she saw as his unthinking support for British foreign policy. She, on the other hand, was seen as 'mentally and emotionally incapable of thinking clearly on this issue because of her close links with the Latins.' And in any other Foreign Service it would have been Mr Haig who had the final word — but not in the United States, where Mrs Kirkpatrick retained the support and confidence of the President, as did, to all appearances, Mr Haig also.[67]

What was to give this schism its critical importance was once again the course of military events.

Having consolidated their sector of the beachhead, men of the Second Batallion of the Parachute Regiment, under the command of Lt. Col. H. Jones (known to the men he commanded simply as H) advanced towards Camilla Creek House and Darwin on 26 and 27 May. They expected to meet with resistance in Darwin when their attack began on 28 May at 2.00 a.m. but it fell with comparative ease. But as Argentine troops retreated into the headland of Goose Green they laid down a barrage of fire from prepared positions, and when at one stage the attack seemed in danger of faltering it was Colonel Jones himself who took charge of a small force to reduce the machine-gun emplacements that were holding it up. Though Colonel Jones was killed in the course of it the action was successful, and by nightfall the British forces were in a commanding position. The next day, 29 May, after a morning of negotiations, the Argentine garrison surrendered, and as they threw down their weapons and webbing the British forces, 600 of them, found that they had defeated and captured 1,400 Argentines, and left 250 dead for the loss of seventeen of their own men.[68]

For reasons of security and because of the slowness of communications, it was two further days before full details of this remarkable victory were known in Britain. Its speed and completeness gave rise to sudden hope, not easily contained, that the fall of Port Stanley itself might be only days away. Certainly with its eye on the gathering diplomatic stormclouds, the Cabinet in London very much hoped that this could be achieved, and gave instructions to that effect.

But to the forces on the ground the difficulties were immense. Advance along the southern route to Bluff Cove involved a painstaking process of eliminating Argentine positions on the hills, but at least there was a dirt road to make the process easier. The northern route to Douglas and Teal Inlet meant struggling across bogland for mile after mile, in strong winds, sub-zero temperatures and the first light snows of winter. Heavy equipment and supplies had to be brought up by helicopter. Unfortunately the loss of the *Atlantic Conveyor* meant a shortage of the heavy-lift Chinooks, and the length of the supply lines and the many uses they were put to stretched the capacity of the lighter machines to the limit.

A sudden strike on Port Stanley across land was therefore impossible. A second landing from the sea north of the capital was considered, and even reported in London as fact,[69] but it was dismissed. With some 9,000 troops in the capital so close at hand, together with a wide range of military radar, missile batteries and rocket launchers, such a landing could speedily have become a massacre. It was judged most prudent to land the 3,500 men of the Fifth Infantry Brigade, transhipped from the *Queen Elizabeth II* to landing vessels in the safety of Grytviken harbour, at the original beach-head at Port San Carlos.[70] Even then, however, the process took time, and though reported correctly to have begun as early as 1 June, was thereafter shrouded in secrecy. The reason was that a Ministry of Defence statement announcing beforehand the imminent attack on Goose Green had aroused great anger among the men of the Second Parachute Regiment, who believed, rightly or wrongly, that it had endangered their lives in the attack, and perhaps cost those of some of their comrades.[71] The Ministry, therefore, took refuge in excessive caution, which allowed rumour and speculation to flourish luxuriantly.

With military operations thus at a critical phase, and with no possibility of a further victory immediately in sight, the British delegation to the United Nations was confronted again at this critical point with pressure for an immediate ceasefire, which would have stalled the repossession of the islands, and, just when so many losses had already been taken, force a compromise. And Mrs Thatcher was in no mood for compromise. To 'hand something to the Argentines', she told Alastair Burnett in an interview on Independent Television News on 2 June, 'to an invader, and an aggressor, and a military dictator, that would not be magnanimity; it would be treachery or betrayal of our own people.'[72]

Yet in Washington President Reagan himself was now talking again of the desirability of a negotiated settlement.[73] So when the same evening in New York Sr Pérez de Cuellar made an interim report to the Security Council, as he had been required to do a week before, and reported no progress, the pressure had built up sufficiently for Spain and Panama to bring forward a resolution calling for an immediate ceasefire. With British artillery now in position on Mount Kent and able to reach Port Stanley at long range[74] there were indications from Argentina not only of its enthusiasm for a ceasefire, but even of its possible preparedness to accept what it had previously rejected: a mutual withdrawal of forces to a predetermined distance. Non-aligned states made every attempt to make their resolution acceptable to Britain, rightly considering that there was little point in putting it forward only to have it vetoed. They therefore added to the ceasefire a call for the simultaneous implementation of Resolution 502, and although the Panamanians, unlike the Spaniards, were originally keen to force a veto by Britain, they were forced to accept the change.[75]

From Britain's point of view, however, the change could not be sufficient to make the resolution acceptable. For over two months the Argentines had ignored the first two parts of Resolution 502, and to be reminded at this stage that the third part — the call for negotiations — was equally applicable to Britain, was like a red rag to a bull. The Cabinet at its meeting on the morning of 4 June therefore proposed what amounted to a complete revision of the resolution to make it absolutely specific, and on its receipt the British delegation in New York realised that there was no chance of getting the necessary changes or postponing a vote, and that they would therefore have to veto it. Stating that the resolution, as proposed, was unacceptable because it did not provide a 'direct and inseparable link between ceasefire and immediate Argentinian withdrawal within a fixed time limit', Sir Anthony cast his vote against. He was supported by Mrs Kirkpatrick for the United States, who thus joined Britain in vetoing the resolution. Nine delegations voted for it: China, Ireland, Japan, Panama, Poland, the Soviet Union, Spain, Uganda and Zaïre. Four abstained: France, Guayana, Jordan and Togo. And then, when the voting was over, the unhappy Mrs Kirkpatrick, who had argued for abstention and had been firmly commanded by Mr Haig to cast her vote against, told the astonished delegates that fresh instructions just in from Mr Haig in Paris had told her after all to abstain. Though the vote could not now be changed, and the veto stood, she wished to place this on record. To compound the disaster she then told reporters that the move had been designed to give the United States the best of both worlds.[76]

President Reagan arrived in Britain on Monday, 7 June, clearly oblivious of the effect that this pantomime might have had on British public opinion. Anti-American opinion was stronger in Britain than in any other European country. Nevertheless for two days he was treated with impeccable politeness as an honoured friend of the family, given a State Banquet at Windsor Castle, accompanied by the Queen herself on a well publicised ride through Windsor Great Park and permitted to address both Houses of Parliament in Westminster Hall. There he embarrassingly called upon Europe to join him in a crusade against the Soviet Union, but redeemed himself to some extent by a public recognition that those who fought for Britain in the Falklands fought 'for a cause, for the belief that armed aggression must not be allowed to succeed, and that the people must participate in the decisions of government under the rule of law.'[77] Nevertheless a keen-eared observer might have detected a very careful choice of words by the Queen when she had welcomed him the previous night at Windsor. 'These past weeks have been testing ones for this country,' she said, 'when once again we have had to stand up for the cause of freedom. The conflict in the Falkland Islands was thrust on us by naked aggression, and we are naturally proud of the way our fighting men are serving their country. But throughout the crisis, we have drawn comfort from the understanding of our position shown by the American people.'[78]

Though it was well known to all who heard these words that the Queen's son, Prince Andrew, was serving with the task force as a helicopter pilot on HMS *Invincible*, by then already claimed sunk three times by Argentine attack, it was not known until after the end of hostilities that, in common with his fellow pilots, one of his duties had been if need be to act as a decoy to incoming missiles, hoping to scatter 'chaff' by a sudden last moment movement to let them explode harmlessly.[79] For all the technology of modern warfare, British success up to that point had had, as in previous wars, to depend more than was comfortable, on the heroism of individuals and the capacity for improvisation.

It was just this capacity for improvisation which was to lead to one of the riskiest moves in the conflict, and one which only just failed to end in a real setback for the British forces. It began with the discovery by Brigadier Tony Wilson, Commander of the Fifth Infantry Brigade, in the course of forward probing from Goose Green, that the telephone line to Bluff Cove had not been cut by retreating Argentines, and that Bluff Cove had been evacuated. Commandeering a Chinook helicopter that had arrived to pick up prisoners, he rushed a hundred men, cradling as many arms as they could carry, to occupy the settlement by nightfall.[80]

The problem then was how to exploit the opportunity. The weather was by now so bad that to reinforce them from San Carlos by land was too slow. The alternative was to do so by sea, using the landing craft *Sir Tristram* and *Sir Galahad*. The first landing, on Sunday 6 June, was successful. But it was detected from Argentine positions on Two Sisters and Sapper Hill, near Stanley, by their sophisticated three dimensional Westinghouse AN/TPS-43 radar, supplied to Argentina by the United States after the ending of President Carter's arms embargo. The second landing was delayed into broad daylight on 7 June by a savage storm, which then cleared, leaving the landing craft clearly visible. Seven hundred men of the Welsh Guards were therefore held back while the Rapier anti-aircraft missiles were disembarked. They were still waiting to disembark close to the shore at 2.00 p.m. when they were attacked without warning from the south, low over the water, by two Skyhawks and two Mirages. *Sir Galahad* was set on fire, and helicopters strove at great risk to rescue dozens of men from the blazing oil. More died when rocket and cannon fire hit *Sir Tristram*. In the circumstances it was amazing that the total death-roll was only fifty, though these figures were deliberately withheld for three days to allow the Argentines in the meantime to believe, which they did easily, that the true figure was nearer 400.[81] Had that been the case, the operations would have received a serious setback. As it was, it did not delay the well-executed night attack on 12 June that captured Two Sisters and Mount Longdon and gave the British forces complete command of all routes leading into and out of Port Stanley. In a statement on the evening of Sunday 13 June Mr Nott was able to say that the advance had been completely successful, though in the course of it HMS *Glamorgan* had been hit by a missile fired from the shore, with the loss of nine lives. 'There is some way still to go, but the outcome is not in doubt', he said.[82]

The end of the fighting came unexpectedly quickly, on the

following morning, when troops starting a further advance held their fire as Argentine forces offered no resistance and white flags appeared in the town. With the key positions of Tumbledown Mountain and Mount William secured to the south-west and Wireless Ridge to the north-west, the position of the garrison was hopeless. In a broadcast from HMS *Fearless* a Spanish-speaking staff officer, Captain Rod Bell, made an appeal to the Argentine commander, General Mario Benjamín Menéndez, to avoid further bloodshed. Though Captain Bell had been calling the local garrison frequency since 7 June he had so far received no reply.

Now, through the •agency of a local doctor, Dr Alison Bleaney, who had heard on the BBC World Service that a safe area was supposed to have been arranged by the Red Cross for civilians and knew that this was not the case, the appeal was brought to the attention of General Menéndez.[83] Within three hours Major General Jeremy Moore, Commander British Land Forces, had negotiated, not just a cease fire, but the surrender of all Argentine forces in both East 14 June (1.00 a.m. BST, 15 June).[84] There was no further fighting. Once again, as at Goose Green, the Argentine troops formed up to lay down their arms, and soon the long lines of prisoners were shuffling through the bitter cold towards the ruined airport, from which subsequently they were to be embarked for repatriation to Puerto Madryn.

Only within two days of the fall of Port Stanley had any hint of what was to come appeared in Argentina itself, and, paralysed by internal conflict and wrangling, the Junta maintained an 'almost farcical' refusal to admit the truth of the surrender.[85] It was Costa Méndez, ironically enough, who was the first to use the word. He also confirmed the existence of a written ceasefire document, having the authority of the Junta.[86] In a last desperate throw to retain his power President Galtieri announced that he would speak to the people from the balcony of the Casa Rosada. But as a huge and angry crowd built up missiles were thrown, the Junta denounced, and newsmen foolish enough to try to interview respondents in English were lucky to escape with only minor injuries. Riot police stormed the crowd and dispersed them, and the President addressed the nation on television.

At times almost shouting at the cameras he told the country: 'The battle for Puerto Argentino [Port Stanley] has ended. Our soldiers fought with supreme effort for the dignity of the nation.' He made no mention of the end of hostilities, but instead asserted that Argentine claims would continue to be pressed until they were achieved, trying vainly to suggest that the war was not lost. 'Defeatism is treason', he asserted.[87]

But he had overplayed his hand. Senior generals met and by seven votes to three voted to end the war. By early on Thursday 17 June, Galtieri was forced to resign. Later the same day he was replaced as a member of the Junta by General Cristino Nicolaides, another right-winger and one equally lacking in any political skill or experience. Even then he was not the first choice: the Chief of Staff, General Vaquero, who was senior, having wisely chosen retirement instead. To compound the chaos the navy refused to accept the resignation of Admiral Anaya, who had precipitated the war in the first place, while Brigadier Lami Dozo, for his part, saw the opportunity for the first time in Argentina's history for the air force to obtain the presidency, in the person of himself. While the Interior Minister, General Alfredo Saint-Jean, took over as interim President, the rivalry both between and within the services precipitated a major political crisis, in which according to reports over the next few days as many as forty different names were actively canvassed for the top job. Finally the navy and air force withdrew from the Junta, and General Reynaldo Bignone, appointed President by the army alone, took office on 1 July amid continued political chaos.[88]

In London the picture was very different. Announcing the surrender Mrs Thatcher made it plain that Britain, having repossessed the islands, was not gong to negotiate with the United Nations or anyone else about their sovereignty. Britain had informed the Argentine Government that it considered hostilities at the South Atlantic to be at an end, and awaited confirmation that this was the case. Britain would certainly 'need the friendliness of other states in the region'. 'If necessary, we have to defend the Falkland Islands alone,' she stated. And in reply to Mr Foot she made her position even clearer:

As to the United Nations resolution, the withdrawal by the Argentines was not honoured and our forces had to go there, because they would not withdraw. Indeed they had to recover and recapture British territory. I cannot agree with the right hon. Gentleman that these men risked their lives in any way to have a United Nations trusteeship. They risked their lives to defend British sovereign territory, the British way of life, and the right of British people to determine their own future.[89]

TABLE 4: British casualties in conflicts since 1945 (servicemen only)

	Place	Year(s)	Dead
1	Korea	1950–1953	537
2	Kenya	1952–1956	537
3	Malaya	1948–1961	525
4	Northern Ireland	1969(–1982)	352*
5	Falkland Islands	1982	255
6	Palestine	1945–1948	223
7	Aden	1964–1967	181
8	Indonesian confrontation	1962–1966	114
9	Cyprus	1954–1959	105
10	Suez	1956	32
11	Oman	1971–1975	24

Sources: adapted from the *Daily Telegraph*, 16 June 1982; *The Times*, 23 June 1982.
*Provisional, to 15 June 1982.

6 Consequences of a crisis

The fall of President Galtieri, it can now be said, marked the end of the Falklands crisis. Did it also, as Mrs Thatcher in her moment of victory seemed to claim, mean the end of the Falkland problem? Was it a fundamental victory for the principles of world order? Or was it merely a further momentary interruption in the collapse of colonialism, as the Latin Americans seem to believe. In the nature of things, it will be a long time until the answers to these and other questions can be known for certain, but in the meantime at least some useful conclusions can be drawn. Let us begin at the beginning.

The most important thing to remember about the Falklands is that they are, first and foremost, a place, and, moreover, a place where people live. They are not, in short, any longer, in Dr Johnson's words, 'a bleak and gloomy solitude, an island thrown aside from human use'.[1] The present inhabitants of the islands have lived there for as much as five generations and, there is every evidence from their own statements, they would like to continue to do so, in their own way. This does not, on the face of it, seem too much to ask. They are colonists in the best sense of that now much misused word: namely, people who have made of a waste land a peaceful, reasonably prosperous and hard-working farming community.

In an interview with Oriana Fallaci, President Galtieri complained that Argentines had not been allowed to settle on the islands. Signorina Fallaci reminded him of his own Italian ancestry — he was the second generation Argentine descendant of immigrants from Genoa and Calabria — and commented: 'So you are colonizers too'.[2]

The fact is that under an Ordinance of 1925, similar to that applied in other British territories of the period, the

Falkland Government did have the power to stop foreigners acquiring land in the islands. Such legislation is not at all unusual, and historically, as in Europe, has been used to protect national security against the threat posed by foreigners buying land close to frontiers or the seashore.[3] The Ordinance was, moreover, used to stop the take-over of the Falkland Islands Company by an Argentine consortium, which would thus have acquired at a stroke the largest share of the islands' land. Historically this special position of the Falkland Islands Company, so reminiscent of the chartered companies that took part in the founding of the American colonies, did by the 1970s appear to be something of an anachronism. Yet in a free-market economy such as that which the Argentine Government was purporting to maintain, it would be hard to argue that there could be any fundamental objection to it. In political terms, however, what it did do was to give a base to an extremely powerful and vocal lobby of islanders in London, who were able to capitalise on the British love of the underdog to argue against any proposal that threatened the traditional pattern of life in the islands.[4] And this meant not only that Argentine development of the islands was resisted, but that until the early 1970s all forms of development involving diversification of the islands' economy were regarded with suspicion and even hostility, as an indication that Britain was trying once again to rid itself of its responsibility for the islands. It was, as they saw it, the British way of life that they were trying to maintain.

The problem, as we have already seen, was that they wished to do so in a world in which decolonisation had been raised to a major principle of the international community.

Here again we hear the voice of Dr Johnson in 1771. 'This was a colony', he wrote, 'which could never become independent, for it never could be able to maintain itself.'[5]

The assumption that the Falklands could never become independent seems, over 200 years later, to have played a major part in limiting thought on the future of the islands. What truth is there in it? From an economic point of view the islands were self-supporting. They could export enough wool and hides to be able to pay for imported goods sufficient to give the islanders a basic if modest standard of living.

Limitations on the standard of living enjoyed by the islanders
stemmed not from their overall capacity to produce but from
the small population, which limited the range of skills and
facilities that could be made available on the islands. The
Argentine forces, drawn as they were mainly from the
greater Buenos Aires area, obviously found it hard to believe
that the islanders would not be attracted by the possibilities
for entertainment and recreation, as well as economic development, of becoming Argentines: they promised them colour
television in time for the World Cup.[6] But, it seems, if the
price of colour television was the loss of their traditional
culture the islanders were prepared to do without. In fact
the small size of the population was an asset and not a
liability, from the economic point of view.

But from a political point of view the position was different. We can dismiss straightaway the argument that, since
there was no other member of the United Nations with so
small a population, the Falklands could not be independent.
Since the late 1960s an increasing number of 'micro-states',
as they are known, have become independent. Nauru, which
became independent in 1968, had a population of under
7,000 at the time.[7] It would be very hard indeed to argue
that a smaller population would find it harder to govern
itself. The reverse is the case. So the only real argument
against the independence of states with very small populations
is that they may, in a world of much larger states, find it
hard, if not impossible, to defend themselves.

In practice, however, this argument, too, is much weaker
than it looks. First of all, there is no reason to suppose that
the threat to small states is a generalised one; that is to say,
that they have to be able to defend themselves against all
comers. There are very few states in the world that really
have the capacity to do that. Others who feel threatened
enter into alliances or seek multilateral guarantees. One,
namely Costa Rica, actually abolished its armed forces in
1948 and since then, despite being twice invaded by its
neighbour Nicaragua, has been able to maintain its independence.[8] In principle, therefore, there is no reason why an
independent Falkland state should not do the same. An
important turning point in the long development of the

Falkland crisis was the decision in 1966 that Britain was not going to be able indefinitely to maintain its commitment to the long-term defence of its outlying territories. Yet as the crisis showed, this was a political decision, not a matter of military necessity. It is quite possible for a state — even one a very long way away — to defend the Falklands for the Falklanders if it wishes to do so, or is prepared to take part in a multilateral system of guarantee.

Independence, however, is not the only option that has not been explored. The other is the integration of the islands with Britain in the fashion of the French overseas *départements*. Here a particularly unfortunate precedent was set by the insensitive handling of the case of Gibraltar.

Gibraltar was ceded to Britain by Spain in 1713 by Treaty and hence is indisputably British territory. The Gibraltarians are passionately pro-British, and, like the Falklanders, want to remain so, but since the Franco period there have been strong right-wing elements in Spain that have demanded the 'return' of Gibraltar. Again, successive British Governments have handled these demands and the requests of Spanish governments, with such a lack of conviction that the Thatcher Government found itself committed to beginning talks with Spain on the future of the Rock just as the Falklands crisis was coming to a head. Yet it is not very long ago that the Gibraltarians actually asked for full integration with the United Kingdom, and were turned down without the matter ever becoming a question for real public debate in Britain.[9]

What it comes down to, in fact, is that the present world order is dominated by land-centred states. As the sad case of Pakistan shows, powerful pressures can be brought to bear to force the disintegration of any state that does not have territorial integrity on land, and there is as yet no evidence that the long trend since the seventeenth century towards the consolidation of states into unified land areas is coming to an end. It is very easy even for island states to accept these assumptions.

But over the four-fifths of the world's surface that consists of water the situation is quite different. Here it is sea communications that unite, instead of dividing. Japan, Indonesia and the Philippines are all states that are joined together by water instead of land, and one of the most striking examples of the possibilities in this respect is the Pacific state of Tuvalu, whose some 10 square miles of land are scattered over more than two million square miles of sea,[10] and yet whose peoples were linked together by their own efforts long before the development of modern mechanical and electrical communications. The British Empire, like the Spanish and Portuguese empires before it, was a sea-borne empire, and in both the Spanish and British Empires there was a brief moment in which the possibility of reconstituting the empire as a federation of democratic self-governing states was canvassed, but for technical reasons not adopted.[11] In our own century, when Heads of State or Heads of Government can fly within hours to present their case in New York before the United Nations, there is no longer any reason why federation, or even integration, over such long distances should not be possible, if thought desirable. Ironically most of the self-governing states formerly part of the British Empire have found it convenient to meet within the framework of the Commonwealth, and for the majority of the Spanish-speaking countries the Organization of American States, as we have seen, offers a forum for expressions of solidarity, and a range of unifying common associations including even reciprocal privileges of citizenship. But there is no reason in principle why various kinds of association, from total independence to total integration, cannot co-exist.

An important factor inhibiting Britain in experimentation has undoubtedly been the notion of 'world opinion' favouring a continued process of decolonisation. Criticism of Britain in this respect by countries of the socialist bloc, including the USSR,[12] has done little to help, and possibly much to hinder the process, which stems from a sense of internal conviction in the first instance. As the quotation above from Dr Johnson shows, written as it was five years before the American Declaration of Independence, the idea of ultimate independence was present in Britain before the bulk of the Empire had even been assembled; it is not a recent phenomenon. But if 'world opinion' has done much to accelerate the process since 1945, there can be no doubt that there is the opinion of one country above all that has formed it. That is the strong and consistent anti-colonial feeling in the United States — 'the first new nation'.[13]

The United States was founded on the principle of the independence and self-government of communities. In the peace settlements after the First World War, in the formation of the United Nations, and in the history of the world since that time, its influence has consistently been exercised in favour of the break-up of the older empires. It has been very successful. The world of today contains well over 150 states. At the same time, economic political and cultural inter-penetration of these states, particularly (though not by any means exclusively) by the two superpowers, the United States and the Soviet Union, has counteracted to some extent the risk of conflict arising from the increase in the number of states claiming sovereignty, which implies, after all, the right to act on their own behalf regardless of others. Both superpowers, moreover, have tended to act in international affairs to conserve their own spheres of interest rather than address themselves to those of their adversary, and the only substantial area in which competition has been free from the overall threat of nuclear war is in the third world and the un-commited states.

Mrs Thatcher has argued that the prime justification of Britain taking military action to resist the Argentine attack on the Falklands was to show that aggression did not pay.[14] Certainly this would be a fundamental principle of any imaginable world order. What surprised observers in the United States, as in other countries, was not that Britain responded to the Argentine attack, but that having put its trust in diplomacy right up to and beyond the moment at which the Argentines came ashore, it then responded so speedily and so forcefully. And this is instructive in a number of ways. First of all it demonstrates how far the assumption had been accepted that the Falklands, as a 'colony', were in some way different from any other British possession, such as the Isle of Man or the Isle of Wight. Secondly it suggests that at any given moment states are viewed by other states as 'aggressive' or 'peace-loving'; a sudden shift from one to the other form of behaviour is considered abnormal, even under provocation. Thirdly, since the willingness to respond is generally associated with the ability to respond, it may imply that Britain's own estimate of her relative powerlessness in the South Atlantic was taken as a fact. Rival conceptions of the use of sea power may well have contributed to this impression.[15]

The rival superpower, the Soviet Union, was equally taken aback by the development of the crisis, taking several days to formulate an appropriate public stance towards it. Thereafter its stereotype of Britain as a colonialist aggressor prevailed not only over the facts of the Argentine attack but also the strongly right-wing anti-Communist orientation of the Argentine government. Persistent reports during the crisis of Soviet intelligence aid to Argentina were subsequently discounted, and in any case it is difficult to see how any useful tactical information could have been made available to Argentina through such a roundabout route. On the contrary, at the crucial point in the development of the crisis when the assurance of Soviet economic support might have had most value to Argentine morale, it became known instead that several months before the USSR had reorientated its purchases of grain for the year towards the United States, and having made its dispositions accordingly would not be in a position to maintain its support to the Argentine economy even if it wanted to do so. The crisis demonstrated therefore that for the Soviet Union the importance of good relations with the United States remained paramount, and that United States ascendancy in Latin America was not again to be challenged from outside.

Above all, however, it must be taken as further evidence that the superpowers see the world as organised primarily in a system of alliances, in which medium-sized powers, such as Britain, are seen primarily if not exclusively as operating within defined regions.[16] In the British case this meant, since the withdrawal from 'East of Suez', the North Atlantic region. This seems natural enough. After all, the system of alliances exists precisely to limit the number of diplomatic possibilities for conflict, and to channel the efforts of competing alliances towards the common struggle. And in the case of the Falklands, as previously in the case of the Middle East, outbreaks of fighting meant an overall loss of security to the United States, caused not just by the struggle between two countries each of which was an ally of the United States, but by extension of representatives of the two major alliance formations which have the United States as their common focus: NATO and the Rio Pact.

The case of the Falklands, I would therefore suggest, represents an unresolved contradiction for the United States between two of its basic principles of foreign policy, between anticolonialism and (since 1947) the construction of a permanent system of alliances. Anticolonialism, by increasing the number of states in the world arena, as well as reducing the capacity of those that are available to form alliances, acts to increase the possibilities for instability. Yet what makes this particularly ironic in the case of the Falklands is the fact that the United States has never previously taken a stand on the ownership of the islands.

Following the action of the captain of the USS *Lexington* in evicting the Buenos Ayrean garrison in 1831, the Administration of President Andrew Jackson consistently refused to support the Argentine claim to the islands, and its successors were to continue to deny any responsibility for his actions. Eventually in 1841 it was Daniel Webster as Secretary of State who took the position that since Britain now possessed the islands under claims dating back long before the incident, the Argentine claims could in effect be postponed indefinitely. In effect he tacitly recognised the British claim, but British sovereignty was never explicitly recognised. As one author put it in 1955: 'The United States has pursued a strict policy of neutrality — even indifference — in the English–Argentine matter.' The same writer, on the other hand, points out that Webster made it quite clear that if a reported British attempt to seize Cuba and abolish slavery there was true, the United States would lend its military resources to Spain.[17]

The policy of the Reagan Administration, taken as a whole, seems then to have been reasonably consistent with this traditional United States position. Hence if it was greeted with some discontent in Britain, it certainly need not have come as any surprise to Argentina. United States policy was not to become involved in the question of sovereignty, which resurfaced at the end of the conflict as something to be discussed between the two contending parties,[18] however unlikely the contingency might be that Britain, in the circumstances, would wish to do so. Mrs Thatcher on her visit to the United States to address the United Nations General Assembly, made it perfectly clear that she would not. At the same time, however, she repeated, as she had done several times, her gratitude to the United States as a 'staunch' ally.[19] While all the evidence is that her gratitude was quite proper and perfectly in order, since United States neutrality on the question of sovereignty did not in any way detract from its official policy of helping Britain to repel armed aggression, it too may reinforce an image that appears to have contributed not a little to the outbreak of the conflict in the first place. I refer to the image of the United States as so powerful that no action can take place anywhere in Latin America without its active or tacit consent.[20]

This image is very widely held in Latin America. On both the left and the right, it is much more satisfying to believe that the United States is responsible for all Latin America's troubles than to believe the responsibility is one's own. But the fact is quite simply that the United States has never had the power to influence events in South America that it has had in the countries of the Caribbean, and even there, in recent years, it has had to learn to live with regimes such as those of Nicaragua and Grenada rather than risk its overall position by being seen to use undue force in its relations with smaller states.

The image of the United States as all powerful is still strong in Britain in the afterglow of the post-war years. As we have seen, Mrs Thatcher, confronted with the first moves in the crisis, did not follow Mr Callaghan's example and send to the Falklands two frigates and a submarine, instead she invoked the aid of President Reagan. Another powerful British myth may also have restrained her: the belief that President Eisenhower stopped the Suez invasion by indicating his displeasure in such a way that a massive run on the pound threatened Britain's very financial stability. If so, it did not happen a second time. Though Britain's financial interests did not appear to be altogether happy about the situation, during the crucial period before the United States came down in support of Britain the pound remained steady and Britain was able to maintain the largest amphibious military operation since the Second World War from start to finish on a fraction of the year's contingency reserve.[21]

This fact, even if known in Latin America, will not convince those who, like the spokesmen for the Argentine Government just before and after the fall of Port Stanley, had the customary excuse ready for their defeat. After all, they argued, they could not have hoped to beat one of the world's leading military powers backed by the power of the United States.[22] Though it is undoubtedly flattering for Britain to be regarded as one of the world's leading military powers, the estimate appears to be correct, and the emphasis on the role of the United States is, for Argentina, self-deception, and wilful self-deception at that. United States logistic support was undoubtedly of great value. But then, if Argentina had not chosen to break the conventions and rules of the international community by launching its invasion in the first place, it too would have had access to much more generous supplies of arms and ammunition during the conflict, and if the United States had from the beginning thrown its weight strongly against Argentina it is quite possible that a peaceful settlement could have been achieved without the necessity for bloodshed. In other words, it seems probable that the Haig Mission, by pre-empting the peace efforts of the United Nations, and depriving Britain of decisive support at the outset, actually made the eventual military escalation of the conflict more rather than less likely.

The result is that two diplomatic lessons of the conflict stand out. Neither gives much comfort to those who believe in a peaceful world of cooperative states working through international agencies.

The first is that *aggression pays*. In the end, Britain proved to be much more aggressive than Argentina; that was decisive. The other is that *intransigence pays*. By reiterating their 'rights' to the Falklands, the Argentines actually succeeded in convincing most of the rest of the world that they were right. They even, it seems, succeeded in causing a series of internal reviews of the position in the British Foreign Office, so that at any given stage of the negotiations the British negotiators were actually much less secure of their position than their public statements suggested. By displaying an equal degree of intransigence on its part, the British Government in 1982 succeeded in coming out of the conflict in a much stronger position than it had been since 1966. The rights of the islanders to be consulted, wholly ignored by Resolution 2065, had been placed back in the centre of the political arena, and in the aftermath of the conflict it looked as though some real attempt might be made at last to inject capital into the islands and complete some of the unfinished starts of the past. The commissioning of the second Shackleton Report was an obvious first step. This time it was unlikely to be the last. And by grasping the nettle and talking clearly about the possibility of independence for the islands, the British Government was taking at least one route previously untried which would lead them out of the dilemma between decolonization and Argentine colonization.[23]

Nor are the military lessons altogether encouraging.

Many wars, like the contemporary Gulf War, take place between states or alliances of roughly equal capacity. But the forces engaged in the Falklands were very different in kind. The British forces consisted of regular soldiers, professionally trained, with experience of no fewer than ten campaigns since the Second World War. The Argentine forces included a core of well-trained troops, but the bulk were conscripts, many it seems called up at short notice. Though the officers had had recent experience of counter-insurgency in their own country (as indeed had the British forces), they had had no experience since 1870 of a war against well-trained regular forces from another nation state with all the resources of a national economy behind them. Only Brazil of all the Latin American states sent ground troops to the Second World War.[24] The shock of the experience, in which they acquitted themselves with gallantry, was a major factor in the Brazilian army's decision in 1964 to take over power and hold it for long enough effectively to develop the country. When this decision came in Argentina it was only at second-hand.

The military officers were, in Feit's phrase, 'armed bureau-crats',[25] accustomed to high status and terrified obedience, and strikingly unwilling to share the hardships of their men — something that is axiomatic in well-trained regular forces. Nor did they cooperate with their rival services. It was the Argentine army that lost the war that their navy had forced on them, and which their air force tried, at the cost of their own lives, to save.

The land war, on paper, should have been much more even than it was. Both armies were reasonably comparable in size. The Argentines were well armed with a wide range of weapons purchased from Britain, Europe and the United States. Military tactics were surprisingly similar to those of the Second World War — the main improvement being in the extensive use of helicopters to assist rapid movement over difficult terrain. But morale among the Argentine con-scripts was strikingly bad, and only at Goose Green does there seem to have been a really effective use of defensive tactics, the high ground around Port Stanley being yielded unexpectedly easily with inevitably disastrous consequences.

It was in the air and at sea that the real changes had occurred. The struggle for the Falklands was the first naval conflict to be fought since 1945, and the first in which missiles were used. The speed with which they travelled, the devastation they caused, and above all the rapid and uncontrollable spread of fire and smoke despite the discipline and training of the men on board all combined to inflict wholly disproportionate loss of life and create a series of spectacular 'victories' for Argentina. Yet in the end they were quite unable to turn the tide. Having suffered only one major loss, no less unexpected however, the Argentine navy then played only a small part in the subsequent conflict, while on the British side the Royal Navy had no alternative if the landings, once begun, were to be carried through and sup-ported up to the moment of ultimate success. Even then, the attack on HMS *Glamorgan* demonstrated that even when air superiority had been achieved, modern warships remained alarmingly vulnerable.[26] Designed to operate in the North Atlantic, under the shelter of ground based radar and air cover, the vessels of the task force had to supply all their own, and in the circumstances it may well be that they were very lucky not to suffer even greater losses.

The question thus must be raised: what if a similar situation arises again? Mr Nott's decision to issue his White Paper after the conflict, essentially unaltered, stemmed from two convictions: that Britain's future defence depended on maintaining an effective seaborne nuclear deterrent force, and that the huge costs could be met by the shift of resources away from conventional warfare capability which would still remain adequate outside the North Atlantic area. There were, and are, three problems with this argument apart from the problem of vulnerability to missile attack.

In the first place the argument seems to assume that Britain's need for overseas power stems only from having to defend colonies. Since the number of colonies is diminishing, the need for overseas power can be expected in the near future to drop and its availability become only a desirable option. The Falkland crisis has dealt this argument a deadly blow, by reminding us of the very many points of land dotted round the globe where a British naval presence may still be needed, and which there is no likelihood of shedding. It was wholly fitting that the crisis, which began with the landing of the 'scrap merchants' on South Georgia, was formally terminated militarily by the surrender on 20 June of eleven Argentine naval personnel on the island of Southern Thule, the southernmost of the South Sandwich Islands. This fulfilled a promise made by Mrs Thatcher in the House of Commons to remove all Argentine military from the Falkland Islands and the Dependencies. The eleven were the staff of a weather station that had been set up by Argentina on the volcanic island in 1976. Repeated protests had been made by Britain after it had been discovered in 1978, but the weather station had not been removed. Its removal was entirely peaceful, the staff surrendering on the approach of the British landing party.[27] As the decision, announced in the middle of the crisis, of the Brazilian Government to build an air base on its island of Trinidade in the South Atlantic shows, odd rocks of this kind may well turn out in the future to have important strategic uses.[28] Their possession harms nobody and, besides, each is surrounded by 200 miles or so of sea which could be much more valuable than the land itself. Looking at the world from the sea has economic as well as strategic uses.

Most dramatically, the announcement on 1 July 1982 by the Guatemalan Government that, with the news of the Falkland crisis still fresh, it was nevertheless disowning the Heads of Agreement with Britain under which Belize obtained independence, was the most striking warning that Britain may yet be called upon to implement existing commitments to defend territories outside the NATO area, whether independent or not. This has implications not only for Britain's ground and air forces in Belize, but also, for example, for its substantial naval commitment to the Indian Ocean and the Gulf region. Nor can such commitments necessarily be handed over to others. In recent years the United States has adopted an attitude towards Guatemalan claims on Belize as equivocal as its attitude towards Argentina's claims on the Falklands, and as the crisis has shown, the interests of even the closest allies are never quite identical.

There can, secondly, be other reasons why a government should need to project power overseas than the possession of colonies. The United States and the Soviet Union have relatively little in the way of overseas colonies. Yet both of them maintain very large navies. Their submarines roam the Polar icecaps as freely as they do the waters of the Line. Their intelligence-gathering vessels form a considerable extension of their capacity to gather valuable and possibly vital strategic information. And the maintenance of their world position involves the ability to project forces overseas: the Soviet Union in Angola and Ethiopia, the United States in Cuba, the Dominican Republic, Vietnam, and the Lebanon. On a more idealistic note, we might also observe that forces have been and may be of even more value to international security if they are used at the request of or under the auspices of an international organisation, in particular the United Nations. This the British response to the Falklands crisis has not helped. Or, as in the case of the Entebbe raid, they may be used in a very restricted way to deal with acts of terrorism or international piracy, which it is difficult to counter in any other way, and impossible if the 'rapid response' is not practicable.

Finally, as regards the question of nuclear deterrence, it is worth noting that here the Falkland conflict marks a milestone which we should do well to ponder. It is the first occasion since 1945 when a nuclear power has been attacked by a non-nuclear power. In view of the fact that (to their eternal credit) no one in Britain at any stage during the crisis suggested using nuclear weapons against Argentina, it seems likely that a conventional attack is more probable, and a nuclear response less probable, than many strategists have thought. If nuclear weapons do not deter when there is no likelihood of effective retaliation, will they do so when there is? Given the dangers involved, the case now seems overwhelming for the nuclear powers to phase out such weapons altogether through balanced reductions.

It is very much in Britain's interests to take an active role in balanced force reductions. One possible interpretation of the Falkland crisis is that modern technology is not just widening the gap between bigger military powers and the rest, it is stretching the whole scale of military possibilities in a way that opens up gaps between medium sized powers such as Britain and the superpowers as great as those between the smaller powers and the medium sized ones. It is hard to say, for at the same time the performance of the Argentine air force in the conflict was in some ways contradictory, yet the outcome seems to confirm it. Whichever is the case, however, for a medium sized power balanced force reductions offer the safest line of adjustment to it.

The decision to buy Trident will contribute nothing to such a development. By complicating the diplomacy involved it will make it even more difficult. Its huge cost distorts the balance of possible defence spending, limiting the range of practicable conventional options. It pushes Britain in the direction of making greater use of civilian resources without effectively thinking through the reorientation of national life that would be necessary to make that effective, even where (as in the case of the task force itself) it is both desirable and practicable. It puts arguments in the hands of opponents of defence spending who argue, with great cogency, that the world order would be much safer if the money were spent instead on the economic development of the Third World. It is certainly important that the lessons of the Falklands crisis should be digested carefully, as Mr Nott proposed. But it will be potentially disastrous if Britain's defence posture is already so rigid that it cannot be altered, for the one thing that is certain in an uncertain world is that change is inevitable.

The final lesson is that defence is much cheaper than the war that follows a successful attack. After 1 April 1982 the possibility of a future Argentine attack cannot be ignored. But with the advantages of a land based missile system and a good airfield, the cost of the defence of the Falklands, even if it were to continue to fall on Britain alone for the foreseeable future, would not be great. It was the need to repossess the islands that was so costly, most particularly in irreplaceable lives.

This is particularly important, since it is in the highest degree improbable that any foreseeable Argentine Government will enter into a formal agreement with Britain to end the state of hostilities that Britain, immediately after the fall of Port Stanley, unilaterally declared to be at an end. It is even less likely — if that were imaginable — that a treaty or other formal agreement can be arrived at between the two countries which will give an Argentine guarantee of non-interference in the future. Yet there are many people who hold that the development of peace involves something more than the mere ending of war. If Argentina will not renounce its claims, can a real peace be achieved?

In theory, no, perhaps. In practice, probably yes. After all, the root cause of the 1982 crisis can be traced back at least to 1771, when the British Government of the day held, in the words of Edmund Burke, 'that the claims on either side are so equivocal and uncertain, as to afford room for endless discussion, while the question of moral or legal right may be for ever unsettled'.[29] At that time, Dr Johnson argued in favour of ignoring the issue of sovereignty. 'Is the King of *France* less a sovereign,' he demanded, 'because the King of *England* partakes his title?'[30] But under the international law of 1982 the islanders have the right to determine their own fate, regardless of past history, and since they pose no threat to Argentine national interests, there is on the face of it no reason why, if the Argentine Government were prepared to face up to those national interests and to inform their people of how they have been misled in the past, a relationship of mutual respect and trust might not grow up of its own accord. Since the time of Perón the Argentine people, and, it seems even British residents in Argentina, have been living in a dream of national glory quite unrelated to the facts of world power or even of their position within Latin America. In the heady aftermath of the Falklands crisis, it will be no less important that Britain does not fall into the self-same trap, but for Britain the experience has probably been too unusual and too brief to cause it to do so.

Britain will be easily forgiven by the rest of Latin America. Not that it will necessarily need it. Argentine dreams of grandeur have not made it popular, and it will not just be in the Itamaratí that the British response will have brought diplomatic benefits. But there are hard lessons for Britain here too.

The most obvious is that Britain must stop ignoring Latin America. It is as near to Britain as is Africa, yet relatively neglected. Cost cutting in schools is driving the Spanish language itself in Britain into the status of a 'minority language'. At University level government cuts have imperilled years of work to promote better relations through academic study — something much valued in Latin America — and faced Latin American students with fees much higher than those offered by some of the leading academic institutions of the United States — or the Soviet Union.[31] The Overseas Service of the BBC, the envy of many other nations, is starved of the small funds that could enormously extend its work. In a dangerous world, only a substantial increase in funds devoted to this task of education can hope to save Britain from the effects of many more problems of understanding and being understood by other cultures, some of which could have much more serious consequences than the evident failure to understand that of Argentina, a country with which in the past Britain has had so much to do.[32]

Lastly, it was the very qualities of determination and single-mindedness that have been characteristic of the British Government under Mrs Thatcher that brought it military success in the South Atlantic. But this success could not have been achieved without cooperation between all those who brought the task force together, and the lesson of that success, therefore, is that British cooperation was successful over Argentine internal conflict. The future of the Thatcher Government will depend on which it chooses to employ in meeting its many other challenges. So too will the future of Argentina.

Appendix:
Security Council Resolution 502

The Security Council, recalling the statement made by the President of the Security Council at the 2,345th meeting of the Security Council on April 1, 1982 (S–14944), calling on the governments of Argentina and the United Kingdom of Great Britain and Northern Ireland to refrain from the use or threat of force in the region of the Falkland Islands (Islas Malvinas), is deeply disturbed at reports of an invasion on April 2, 1982, by armed forces of Argentina, determining that there exists a breach of the peace in the region of the Falkland Islands (Islas Malvinas):

1) Demands an immediate cessation of hostilities:
2) Demands an immediate withdrawal of all Argentine forces from the Falkland Islands (Islas Malvinas):
3) Calls on the governments of Argentina and the United Kingdom to seek a diplomatic solution to their differences, and to respect fully the purposes and principles of the Charter of the United Nations.

Notes

Chapter 1

1. The line runs between 48° and 49° west of Greenwich. C. H. Haring, *The Spanish Empire in America* (New York, Harcourt Brace and World, 1952), p. 7 n.
2. A witty reference to the Requerimiento of 1503, for which see Lewis Hanke, 'The *Requerimiento* and its Interpreters', *Revista de Historia de América*, I, 1937, p. 28, cited in Haring, p. 7.
3. J. G. Starke, *Introduction to International Law* (London, Butterworth's, 1967) pp. 156-7. Frederick H. Hartmann, *The Relations of Nations* (New York, Macmillan, 1962), p. 688 (Appendix B: Charter of the United Nations).
4. Details of early exploration and settlement are given in The Annual Register (henceforth cited as AR) 1771, pp. 1 ff. If Davis's sighting is discounted, the right of first discovery would lie with the Dutchman Sebald de Weert of the *Geloof*, January 1600.
5. ibid., pp. 9-11.
6. AR 1774, p. 147.
7. Thomas B. Davis, Jr., *Carlos de Alvear; Man of Revolution* (Durham, NC, Duke University Press, 1955), pp. 98-108.
8. AR 1833, pp. 307-9; pp. 371-5 of Chronicle reprints documents.
9. Central Office of Information, *The Falkland Islands and Dependencies* (London, 1973) (henceforth COI Factsheet), pp. 1-2.
10. Starke, pp. 157-8, see also J. E. S. Fawcett, 'The Falklands and the Law', *The World Today*, June 1982, p. 204.
11. *The Sunday Times*, 20 June 1982.
12. The definitive study of the early history of Argentine claims is Julius Goebel, *The Struggle for the Falkland Islands* (New Haven, Conn., Yale University Press, 1982 — first published 1927), but as J. C. J. Metford points out, his conclusions, contradicted by his facts, are quite incorrect. See also J. C. J. Metford, 'Falklands or Malvinas? The background for the dispute', *International Affairs*, XLIX, No. 3, July 1968, pp. 463-481.
13. Haring, p. 71.
14. Starke, p. 159, who also discusses the so-called 'sector theory', for which see George I. Blanksten, *Perón's Argentina* (New York, Russell and Russell, 1965 — first published 1953).

15. A point made by the Falkland Islands Committee, 'The Falkland Islands: the Facts . . . and the Figures' (London, 1974, mimeo).
16. COI Factsheet.
17. *Encyclopaedia Britannica*, 13th edn., s.v. 'Falkland Islands'.
18. COI Factsheet.
19. Figures from 1982 Census.
20. COI Factsheet.
21. ibid.
22. *Encyclopaedia Britannica*, 13th edn., Supplement, s.v. 'Falkland Islands, Battle of the'.

Chapter 2

1. A useful introduction to Argentine history is George Pendle, *Argentina* (London, Oxford University Press for Royal Institute of International Affairs, 1961). A more detailed treatment can be found in James Scobie, *Argentina: a City and a Nation* (New York, Oxford University Press, 1964).
2. There are many Argentine biographies of Rosas. A sensational book in English that draws parallels between his career and that of Perón is Fleur Cowles, *Bloody Precedent: the Perón Story* (London, Frederick Muller, 1952).
3. David Rock, ed., *Argentina in the Twentieth Century* (London, Duckworth, 1975).
4. Blanksten, p. 307. For the Perón period see also Arthur P. Whitaker, *Argentina* (Englewood Cliffs, NJ, Prentice-Hall, 1964), pp. 104–50.
5. Blanksten, pp. 47–9.
6. ibid., pp. 69–71.
7. ibid., ch. 7, pp. 87 ff., and Marysa Navarro, 'Evita's Charismatic Leadership', in Michael Conniff, ed., *Latin American Populism in Comparative Perspective* (Albuquerque, University of New Mexico Press, 1982), pp. 47–66.
8. AR 1948, pp. 3, 353.
9. *The Times*, 19 January 1949.
10. AR 1955, p. 144.
11. Arthur P. Whitaker, *Argentine Upheaval: Perón's Fall and the new Regime* (London, Atlantic Press, 1956); AR 1955, pp. 328–9.
12. AR 1966, pp. 191–3; see also Edwin Lieuwen, *General versus Presidents: Neomilitarism in Latin America* (London, Pall Mall, 1964), pp. 10–25, for the fall of Frondizi and an assessment of the Argentine military.
13. AR 1973, pp. 91–2.
14. *The Times*, 2 July 1974; AR 1974, pp. 97–8.

15. Blanksten, p. 79.
16. Bank of London & South America (henceforth (BOLSA) *Review*, March 1976; *The Times*, 25, 26, 27 and 30 March 1976; AR 1976, pp. 80-1.
17. *The Times*, 5 February 1980.
18. On the Videla period see Simon Collier, 'Argentina: Travail and Censure', *International Affairs*, LVII, No. 3, summer 1981, pp. 477-81 and Charles Maechling, Jr., 'The Argentine Pariah', *Foreign Policy*, No. XLV, winter 1981-2, pp. 69-83.
19. Arrigo Levi, 'Argentine Junta lays down conditions for a return to democracy', *The Times*, 26 and 30 June 1980.
20. Quoted in Pendle, p. 178.
21. E. M. Borchard, 'Calvo and Drago Doctrines', *Encyclopedia of the Social Sciences* (New York, Macmillan, 1930) III, pp. 153-6.
22. ibid.
23. Bryce Wood, *The United States and Latin American Wars, 1932-1942* (New York, Columbia University Press, 1966), pp. 101-5, 115 ff.
24. Sir Thomas Holditch, *The Countries of the King's Award* (London, Hurst and Blackett, 1904).
25. AR 1978, pp. 70-2.
26. *The Times*, 13 December 1980.
27. Blanksten, pp. 280-98.
28. Pendle, p. 179; BOLSA *Fortnightly Review*, 30 March 1957, p. 235.
29. *The Times*, 3 April 1982.
30. Chronology 1964-75 follows UK Government, Foreign Office, 'Background Paper for Meeting on Falkland Islands, 8 May 1975' (mimeo) (henceforth 'Background Paper'); see also Martin Walker, 'The Give-Away Years', *Guardian Weekend*, 19 June 1982.
31. *The Times*, 17 December 1965.
32. 'Background Paper'; Walker, *Guardian Weekend*, 19 June 1982.
33. *The Times*, 3 April 1982.
34. 'Background Paper'; *The Times*, 14 March 1968.
35. *The Times*, 28 March 1968.
36. See Walker, *Guardian Weekend*, 19 June 1982, for details of Lord Chalfont's role, and his warning of the possibility of Argentine attack.
37. *The Times*, 22 and 25 November 1969.
38. See below, p. 47.
39. *The Times*, 2 January and 30 June 1969.
40. AR 1969, p. 181.
41. *The Guardian*, 9 June 1980.

42. *The Sunday Times*, 31 May 1970; *The Guardian*, 18 July 1970.
43. *The Times*, 15 June 1970; *The New York Times*, 15 June 1970.
44. AR 1971, p. 81.
45. *The Economist*, 26 August 1972.
46. For a critique of the effects of the Agreement see E. W. Hunter Christie, *Report* (London, Falkland Islands Committee, April 1975).
47. 'Background Paper'.
48. AR 1973, pp. 91–2.
49. See also AR 1973, p. 381, on the Non-Aligned Countries' declaration on the right to independence of territories in Latin America.
50. *The Times*, 4 October 1973.
51. AR 1974, p. 97.
52. AR 1975, p. 82.
53. *The Times*, 15 September, 1975.
54. *Prensa Latina* bulletin No. 567.
55. AR 1976, p. 80.
56. BOLSA *Review*, June 1976.
57. Walker, *Guardian Weekend*, 19 June 1982; see also *The Times*, 26 July 1974.
58. *The Times*, 6, 14, 18 and 19 February 1976; 12 March 1976.
59. *Economic Survey of the Falkland Islands* (London, HMSO, 1976).
60. Colin Phipps, *What Future for the Falklands?* Fabian Tract 450 (London, Fabian Society, July 1977), p. 9; *Neue Zürcher Zeitung*, 10 July 1970; *The Times*, 7 April 1982.
61. *The Times*, 17, 19, 22, 23, and 24 February; 23 March; 27 April 1977.
62. *The Times*, 5 April 1982.
63. Now part of the Coalite Group.
64. *The Times*, 23 June 1978; *International Herald Tribune*, 2 July 1978.
65. BOLSA *Review*, December 1979.
66. *The Times*, 29 April; 18, 24 and 28 November; 1 December 1980.
67. John J. Johnson, *The Military and Society in Latin America* (Stanford, Cal., Stanford University Press, 1964); Edwin Lieuwen, *Arms and Politics in Latin America* (New York, Praeger, 1963) esp. pp. 66–74.
68. *The Statesman's Year Book . . . 1981–82*, ed. John Paxton (London, Macmillan, 1981), p. 90.
69. *The Times*, 3 May 1982.
70. *The Times*, 25 May 1982.
71. Peter Calvert, 'The Coup: a critical restatement', *Third World Quarterly*, I, 4, October 1979, pp. 89–96.

72. *The Times*, 12 February 1976. The country was Ecuador; the President was General Rodríguez Lara. The request was granted.

73. AR 1955, p. 328.

74. *The Times*, 30 March 1981.

75. *The Times*, 6 June 1981.

76. Summary of history of the dispute in *The Times*, 20 April 1982.

77. *Keesing's Contemporary Archives*, XXVII, 1981, 30981A.

78. *The Economist*, 28 November 1981, p. 50; BOLSA *Review*, November 1981, pp. 190–5.

79. *The Times*, 6 May 1982.

80. *The Times*, 21 November 1981.

81. ibid.; BOLSA *Review*, February 1982.

82. *The Economist*, 28 November 1981, p. 50, and 19 December 1981, p. 63; 'Simple soldier holds key to war or peace', *The Times*, 16 April 1982.

83. Tony Emerson, 'How the General fell into the Falklands trap', *The Times*, 22 April 1982.

84. ibid.

85. *Time*, 15 April 1982.

86. *The Times*, 30 April 1982.

87. *The Guardian*, 25 February and 5 March 1982; *The Times*, 6 April 1982.

88. *The Times*, 3 March 1981.

89. *The Times*, 27 February 1981.

90. *The Times*, 16 April 1982.

91. BBC TV interview, 2 April 1982.

92. *The Times*, 24, 29 and 30 March 1982.

93. *The Guardian*, 6 April 1982.

94. *The Guardian*, 5 April 1982.

95. *The Times*, 5 April 1982.

96. *The Times*, 6 April 1982.

Chapter 3

1. On British pragmatism see Joseph Frankel, *British Foreign Policy, 1945–75* (London, OUP for RIIA, 1975), pp. 112–17.

2. Anthony Nutting, *No End of a Lesson; the Story of Suez* (London, Constable, 1967). See also David Carlton, 'The Suez parallels that could swamp Mrs Thatcher', *The Times*, 15 May 1982.

3. *The Times*, 1 March 1963.

4. Harold Wilson, *The Labour Government, 1964–1970* (London, Weidenfeld & Nicholson and Michael Joseph, 1971), p. 461.

5. ibid., pp. 178–83 and *passim*.

6. ibid., pp. 693-6.

7. Nora Beloff, *The General says No* (Harmondsworth, Penguin Books, 1963).

8. *The United Kingdom Defence Programme: The Way Forward*, Cmnd. 8288 (London, HMSO, 1981); *The Economist*, 25 July 1981, p. 55; 5 December 1981, p. 74.

9. *Statement on the Defence Estimates 1982*, Pt. 1. Cmnd. 8529-1 (London, HMSO, 1982), par. 229, p. 16.

10. *Times Guide to the House of Commons, July 1979*. See also, *inter alia*, profile by Julian Critchley in *The Times*, 21 June 1982.

11. *The Times*, 5 April 1982.

12. *The Times*, 21 December 1979; cf. *The Sunday Times*, 6 January 1980.

13. *The Times*, 6 April 1982.

14. For effects of regrouping, see Walker, *Guardian Weekend* 19 June 1982. On FCO see William Wallace, *The Foreign Policy Process in Britain* (London, RIIA, 1975), pp. 23-34; Robert Boardman & A. J. R. Groom, eds., *The Management of Britain's External Relations* (London, Macmillan, 1973), pp. 31-73.

15. Peter Calvert, 'Guatemala and Belize', *Contemporary Review*, CCXXVIII, No. 1320, January 1976, pp. 7-12.

16. *The Economist*, 23 May 1981, pp. 29-30.

17. Portrait of John Nott in *The Times*, 17 June 1982.

18. *The Times*, 21 June 1982; *The Sunday Times*, 20 June 1982.

19. *The Times*, 18 June 1982; 24 March 1982.

20. UK Parliament: House of Commons, *Official Report* (henceforth *Off. Rep.*) 1237, 23 March 1982, cc. 798-9.

21. *The Times*, 2 April 1982.

22. Simon Winchester, 'How Falklands were invaded', *The Times*, 3 April 1982.

23. ibid.

24. *The Times*, 3 April 1982.

25. *Off. Rep.* 1239, 2 April 1982, cc. 571, 573.

26. ibid., cc. 571-2.

27. ibid., c. 572.

28. *The Guardian*, 5 April 1982.

29. *The Times*, 3 April 1982.

30. *Off. Rep.* 1239, 3 April 1982, c. 634.

31. ibid., c. 636.

32. ibid., cc. 639, 641.

33. ibid., cc. 650, 667.

34. *The Times*, 5 April 1982.

35. Full text in *The Times*, 15 April 1982 — see Appendix.

36. Fawcett, *World Today*, June 1982.
37. *The Guardian*, 5 April 1982.
38. *The Times*, 6 April 1982.
39. *The Times Guide to the House of Commons, July 1979*; profile by Julian Critchley in *The Times*, 24 May 1982.

Chapter 4

1. *The Times*, 8 April 1982; David Watt, 'A few home truths from the South Atlantic', *The Times*, 16 April 1982.
2. *The Times*, 3 April 1982.
3. *The Times*, 6 April 1982.
4. *The Times*, 7 April 1982; 5 April 1982. A list of the ships in the force appeared in *The Times* on 10 and 21 April 1982.
5. *The Times*, 8 April 1982.
6. *The Times*, 7 April 1982.
7. *The Times*, 23 April 1982.
8. *The Times*, 7 and 10 April 1982.
9. *The Times*, 8 April 1982.
10. *The Times*, 5 April 1982; *Off. Rep.*, 1239, 3 April 1982, c. 646.
11. *The Times*, 10 April; 12 April 1982.
12. *Off. Rep.*, 1239, 7 April 1982, c. 960.
13. ibid., cc. 965-6, 968-9.
14. *The Times*, 8 April 1982.
15. ibid.
16. Mr Haig resigned as Secretary of State on 25 June 1982; see BBC News, 25 June 1982; *Daily Telegraph*, 26 June 1982.
17. *The Times*, 10 April 1982.
18. ibid.
19. *The Times*, 12 April 1982.
20. ibid.
21. *Time*, 26 April 1982.
22. *The Times*, 13 April 1982.
23. *Time*, 26 April 1982; *The Times*, 14 April 1982.
24. *The Times*, 14 April 1982.
25. *Off. Rep.*, 1240, 14 April 1982, cc. 1146 ff.
26. *The Times*, 15 April 1982.
27. *The Times*, 14 April 1982.
28. ibid.
29. *The Times*, 16 April 1982.
30. *The Times*, 17 April 1982.
31. *The Times*, 16 April 1982.
32. ibid., *The Guardian*, 5 April 1982; for Venezuelan claims, see *The Times*, 18 June 1982.

33. *Time*, 26 April 1982.
34. *The Times*, 17 April 1982.
35. *Time*, 26 April 1982.
36. *The Times*, 19 April 1982.
37. *The Times*, 20 April 1982.
38. ibid. The orders to leave port were given by Admiral Anaya on 15 April and countermanded by the Junta, see *The Times*, 6 May 1982.
39. *The Times*, 20 April 1982.
40. *Time*, 26 April 1982.
41. *Off. Rep.*, 1240, 20 April 1982, c. 119.
42. ibid., cc. 119–20, 122.
43. *The Times*, 22 April 1982.
44. *Off. Rep.*, 1240, 21 April 1982, cc. 271, 273.
45. ibid., cc. 278, 280.
46. *Off. Rep.*, 1240, 22 April 1982, cc. 417, 419.
47. *The Times*, 26 April 1982.
48. *The Times*, 23 April 1982.
49. *The Times*, 24 April 1982.
50. *The Times*, 23 April 1982.
51. *The Sunday Times*, 6 June 1982.
52. *The Times*, 26 and 27 April 1982.
53. *The Times*, 26 April 1982.
54. Gordon Connell-Smith, *The Inter-American System* (London, OUP, 1966); O. Carlos Stoetzer, *The Organization of American States: an Introduction* (New York, Praeger, 1965).
55. Calvert, *Latin America*, pp. 145–6.
56. *The Times*, 3 and 4 February 1981; for the background see Wood, pp. 255 ff.
57. *Lima Times*, 7 May 1982; *The Times*, 5 May 1982.
58. *Keesing's Contemporary Archives*, 30317A.
59. *The Times*, 28 April 1982.
60. Full text in *The Times*, 29 April 1982.
61. *The Times*, 29 April 1982.
62. *The Times*, 6 May 1982.
63. *The Times*, 27 April 1982.
64. *Off. Rep.* 1241, 27 April 1982, cc. 719–21.
65. *The Times*, 29 April 1982.
66. *Off. Rep.*, 1241, 29 April 1982, c. 182.
67. ibid., cc. 182–3.
68. *The Times*, 1 May 1982.
69. ibid.
70. ibid.
71. ibid.
72. *The Sunday Times*, 2 May 1982.

Chapter 5

1. *The Sunday Times*, 2 May 1982.
2. BBC TV News; *The Times*, 17 June 1982.
3. *The Sunday Times*, 20 June 1982.
4. *The Times*, 3 May 1982.
5. ibid.
6. *The Times*, 4 and 5 May 1982; *The Sunday Times*, 4 July 1982.
7. *The Times*, 5 May 1982.
8. ibid., '400 rescued from cruiser, junta says'.
9. ibid., 'W. Germany calls for a ceasefire'.
10. ibid., 'Haig sees intransigence rising'.
11. ibid., 'HMS *Sheffield* hit and sunk; Harrier shot down'.
12. *The Times*, 6 May 1982.
13. ITN News
14. *The Times*, 5 and 6 May 1982.
15. *The Times*, 7 May 1982.
16. *Off. Rep.*, 1242, 4 May 1982, c. 31.
17. ibid., c. 16.
18. *Off. Rep.*, 1242, 5 May 1982, c. 161.
19. *The Times*, 7 May 1982, 'Britain seen in US as on defensive'.
20. *The Times*, 6 and 7 May 1982; see also the subsequent Peruvian statement of the plan, *The Times*, 10 May 1982.
21. *The Times*, 7 May 1982.
22. *Off. Rep.*, 1243, 7 May 1982, c. 394; 1242, 6 May 1982, c. 280.
23. *The Times*, 8 May 1982.
24. *The Times*, 7 May 1982.
25. *Off. Rep.*, 1343, 7 May 1982, cc. 394, 395, 397.
26. *The Times*, 8 May 1982.
27. But see also the comments of Professor Colonel Gerald Draper, *The Times*, 7 April 1982.
28. *The Times*, 10 and 11 May 1982; BBC News.
29. ibid.
30. *The Times*, 12 May 1982.
31. *The Times*, 10 May 1982.
32. *The Times*, 13 May 1982.
33. *The Times*, 14 May 1982.
34. *The Times*, 15 May 1982.
35. ibid.
36. *The Guardian*, 14 May 1982.
37. ibid.
38. *Off Rep.*, 1243, 13 May 1982, cc. 942–3, 952 ff., esp. cc. 965, 966, 961, 985.
39. ibid., c. 954.

40. *The Times*, 17 May 1982.
41. *The Times*, 15 May 1982; BBC TV News.
42. *The Times*, 19 June 1982.
43. *The Times*, 17 May 1982.
44. *The Times*, 18 May 1982.
45. *The Times*, 19 May 1982.
46. *The Times*, 18 May 1982.
47. ibid.
48. *The Times*, 19 May 1982.
49. *Off. Rep.*, 1244, 20 May 1982, c. 477.
50. ibid., cc. 478-81, 488, 559-61; *The Times*, 22 May 1982.
51. *The Sunday Times*, 23 May 1982, indicates clearly that the Argen-
    tines did not consider negotiations ended. Tony Emerson, 'Why the
    doves too are angered by "Señora No"', *The Times*, 28 May 1982,
    argues that the British position seemed from Buenos Aires to
    harden, leaving the 'doves' without support.
52. *The Times*, 15 May 1982.
53. *The Times*, 22 May 1982; *The Sunday Times*, 23 May 1982.
54. *The Sunday Times*, 30 May 1982.
55. ITN News: 'The Taking of the Falklands', 19 June 1982.
56. *The Times*, 12 June 1982; see also on aluminium risk *The Times*,
    25 May 1982.
57. *The Times*, 12 June 1982; interview with General Jeremy Moore,
    BBC TV, 25 June 1982; cf. *The Sunday Times*, 30 May 1982.
58. *The Sunday Times*, 30 May 1982.
59. *The Times*, 11 June 1982; a report in *The Times*, 5 June 1982,
    earlier said Gabriel anti-ship missiles were known to have been
    delivered from Israel.
60. *The Times*, 27 May 1982.
61. *The Times*, 24 May 1982.
62. *The Times*, 26 May 1982.
63. ibid.
64. *The Times*, 27 May 1982.
65. *The Times*, 28 May 1982.
66. *The Times*, 29 May 1982.
67. *The Times*, 31 May 1982. Jeane Kirkpatrick, *Leader and Vanguard
    in Mass Society: a Study of Peronist Argentina* (Cambridge, Mass.,
    MIT Press, 1971) shows Falklands on map of Argentina, p. 65.
68. *The Times*, 31 May 1982.
69. *The Times*, 1 June 1982: '3000 troops from QE2 "ashore near
    Stanley"'.
70. *The Times*, 7 June 1982. The news was first disclosed in a report
    by Michael Nicholson of ITN screened on 6 June 1982.

71. *The Sunday Times*, 6 June 1982.
72. *The Times*, 3 June 1982.
73. *The Guardian*, 3 June 1982.
74. *The Times*, 3 June 1982.
75. *The Times*, 4, 5 and 9 June 1982.
76. *The Times*, 7 June 1982; *The Sunday Times*, 6 June 1982: ' "Why didn't she eat her new instructions?" moaned a US observer.'
77. *The Times*, 9 June 1982.
78. ibid.
79. ITN News.
80. Michael Nicholson, ITN News, 9 June 1982.
81. *The Sunday Times*, 13 June 1982; *The Times*, 10 June 1982.
82. *The Times*, 14 June 1982.
83. *The Times*, 15 June 1982; *The Sunday Times*, 20 June 1982.
84. *The Times*, 15 June 1982.
85. *The Times*, 17 June 1982.
86. *The Times*, 16 June 1982. Full text of the surrender document in *The Times*, 17 June 1982.
87. *The Times*, 17 June 1982.
88. *The Times*, 22 June 1982; 2 July 1982.
89. *Off. Rep.*, 1247, 15 June 1982, cc. 734, 737, 782.

Chapter 6

1. Samuel Johnson, 'Thoughts on the Late Transactions respecting Falklands Island [1771]', *The Works of Samuel Johnson, LID* (London, J. Buckland *et al.*, 1787), X, p. 56.
2. *The Times*, 12 June 1982.
3. E. W. Hunter Christie, 'Argentinian settlers', *The Times*, 1 June 1982.
4. Walker, *Guardian Weekend*, 19 June 1982.
5. Johnson, p. 44.
6. ITN News.
7. *Statesman's Year Book*, p. 881.
8. Charles D. Ameringer, *Don Pepe; a political biography of José Figueres of Costa Rica* (Albuquerque, University of New Mexico Press, 1978), pp. 75–84.
9. *The Times*, 21 May; 21 and 22 June 1982.
10. *Statesman's Year Book*, p. 1209.
11. Under the abortive Constitution of 1812 all Spanish kingdoms would have had representation in the Cortes.
12. John Hemming, 'Soviet view of the Falklands', *The Times*, 17 May 1982, replying to a letter of Igor Pavlov, published 12 May.

13. Title of book by Seymour Martin Lipset, *The First New Nation: the United States in Historical and Comparative Perspective* (London, Heinemann, 1964).

14. David Watt, 'Now let's shoot down the delusions', *The Times*, 18 June 1982.

15. The US has no fewer than thirteen giant aircraft carriers capable of taking conventional aircraft; the UK has none. See US comment on the value to Britain of even one carrier in *The Times*, 4 June 1982.

16. But see also Frankel, pp. 117-19, for the primacy of Britain's European role to the FO since Sir Eyre Crowe's Memorandum of 1907.

17. Davis, pp. 119-22.

18. *The Times*, 16 and 18 June 1982.

19. BBC News, 24 June 1982.

20. See Peter Calvert, 'Recent Political and Diplomatic Changes in South America', *The International Yearbook of Foreign Policy Analysis*, I, 1973, ed. Peter Jones (London, Croom Helm, 1974).

21. *The Times*, 14 June 1982.

22. Communiqué of the Argentine Joint Chiefs of Staff, quoted in *The Times*, 18 June 1982.

23. *The Times*, 16 June 1982.

24. Frank D. McCann, Jr., *The Brazilian-American Alliance, 1937-45* (Princeton, Princeton University Press, 1973), pp. 403 ff.

25. Edward Feit, *The Armed Bureaucrats, military-administrative regimes and political development* (Boston, Houghton Mifflin, 1973).

26. *The Times*, 17 June 1982.

27. *The Times*, 21 June 1982; *Off. Rep.*, 1247, 15 June 1982, c. 737; 1248, 22 June 1982, c. 76.

28. *The Times*, 5 June 1982.

29. AR 1771, p. 51.

30. Johnson, p. 56.

31. Professor J. Lynch, 'The Anglo-Latin gulf', *The Times*, 14 June 1982.

32. For two examples, see Guillermo Makin, 'Why defeat may not sink Galtieri', *The Times*, 15 June 1982, who pointed out correctly that civilian governments in Argentina are even *more* likely than military ones to pursue the Falklands issue, and the devastating criticisms of *The Times*'s own editorial suggestions on other Latin American problems by Malcolm Deas in *The Times* of 4 June 1982.

Index